Taxcafe.co.uk Tax Guides

Capital Gains Tax

Emergency Tax Planning Guide

By Carl Bayley BSc ACA

Important Legal Notices:

Taxcafe®
TAX GUIDE – "Capital Gains Tax – Emergency Tax Planning Guide"

Published by:
Taxcafe UK Limited
67 Milton Road
Kirkcaldy
KY1 1TL
United Kingdom
Tel: (01592) 560081

First Edition, June 2010

ISBN 978-1-907302-19-0

Copyright
Copyright © Carl Bayley 2010. All rights reserved.

No part of this publication may be reproduced or transmitted in any form or by any means (electronically or mechanically, including photocopying, recording or storing it in any medium by electronic means) without the prior permission in writing of the copyright owner except in accordance with the provisions of the Copyright, Designs and Patents Act 1988 or under the terms of a licence issued by the Copyright Licensing Agency Ltd, 90 Tottenham Court Road, London, W1P 0LP. All applications for the written permission of the copyright owner to reproduce or transmit any part of the Tax Guide should be sent to the publisher.

Warning: Any unauthorised reproduction or transmission of any part of this Tax Guide may result in criminal prosecution and a civil claim for damages.

Trademarks
Taxcafe® is a registered trademark of Taxcafe UK Limited. All other logos, trademarks, names and logos in this Tax Guide may be trademarks of their respective owners.

Disclaimer
Before reading or relying on the content of this Tax Guide, please read carefully the disclaimer on the last page which applies. If you have queries then please contact the publisher at team@taxcafe.co.uk.

About the Author

Carl Bayley is the author of a series of 'Plain English' tax guides designed specifically for the layman. Carl's particular speciality is his ability to take the weird, complex and inexplicable world of taxation and set it out in the kind of clear, straightforward language that taxpayers themselves can understand. As he often says himself, "my job is to translate 'tax' into English".

Carl enjoys his role as a tax author, as he explains: "Writing these guides gives me the opportunity to use the skills and knowledge learned over almost twenty-five years in the tax profession for the benefit of a wider audience. The most satisfying part of my success as an author is the chance to give the average person the same standard of advice as the 'big guys' at a price which everyone can afford."

Carl takes the same approach when speaking on taxation, a role he frequently undertakes with great enthusiasm, including his highly acclaimed annual 'Budget Breakfast' for the Institute of Chartered Accountants.

In addition to being a recognised author and speaker on the subject, Carl has often spoken on taxation on radio and television, including the BBC's 'It's Your Money' programme and BBC Radio 2's Jeremy Vine Show.

Carl began his career as a Chartered Accountant in 1983 with one of the 'Big 4' accountancy firms. After qualifying as a double prize-winner, he immediately began specialising in taxation.

After honing his skills with several major international firms, Carl began the new millennium by launching his own tax and accounting practice, Bayley Miller Limited, through which he provides advice on a wide variety of taxation issues; especially property taxation, Inheritance Tax and tax planning for small and medium-sized businesses.

Carl is a member of the governing Council of the Institute of Chartered Accountants in England and Wales and a former Chairman of ICAEW Scotland. He has co-organised the annual Peebles Tax Conference for the last eight years.

When he isn't working, Carl takes on the equally taxing challenges of hill walking and writing poetry and fiction. Carl lives in Scotland with his partner Isabel and has four children.

Dedication

For the Past,

Firstly, I dedicate this book to the memory of those I have loved and lost:

First of all, to my beloved mother Diana – what would you think if you could see me now? The memory of your love warms me still. Thank you for making it all possible;

To my dear grandfather, Arthur - your wise words still come back to guide me; and to my loving grandmothers, Doris and Winifred;

Between you, you left me with nothing I could spend, but everything I need.

Also to my beloved friend and companion, Dawson, who waited so patiently for me to come home every night and who left me in the middle of our last walk together. Thank you for all those happy miles; I still miss you son.

For the Present,

Above all, I must dedicate this book to the person who stands, like a shining beacon, at the centre of every part of my life: Isabel, my 'life support system', whose unflinching support has seen me through the best and the worst. Whether anyone will ever call me a 'great man' I do not know, but I do know that I have a great woman behind me.

Without her help, support and encouragement, this book, and the others I have written, could never have been.

For the Future,

Finally, I also dedicate this book to four very special young people: Michelle, Louise, James and Robert.

I am so very proud of every one of you and I can only hope that I, in turn, will also be able to leave each of you with everything that you need.

Thanks

First and foremost, I must say an enormous thank you to Isabel: for all her help researching everything from obscure points of tax legislation to popular girls' names in Asia; for reading countless drafts; for making sure I stop to eat and sleep; for putting up with me when I'm under pressure and, most of all, for keeping me company into the 'wee small hours' on many a long and otherwise lonely night. I simply cannot ever thank her enough for everything that she does for me, but I intend to spend the rest of my life trying!

Thanks to the Taxcafe team, past and present, for their help in making these books far more successful than I could ever have dreamed.

I would like to thank my old friend and mentor, Peter Rayney, for his inspiration and for showing me that tax and humour can mix.

And last, but far from least, thanks to Ann for keeping us right!

C.B., Roxburghshire, May 2010

BUSINESS TAX SAVER

If you like this tax guide...

You will also like *Business Tax Saver*...

Our monthly guide to BIG business tax savings

<u>You can try it for just £1</u>

Go to www.taxcafe.co.uk/businesstaxsaver.html

Contents

Introduction	1
Scope of this Guide	4
A Word about the Examples in this Guide	5
Chapter 1 - The 'Current' Capital Gains Tax Regime	6
1.1 Overview	6
1.2 The Flat Rate Regime	6
1.3 Who Pays Capital Gains Tax?	7
1.4 When is Capital Gains Tax Payable?	8
1.5 Exemptions and Reliefs	8
Chapter 2 - Special Cases	11
2.1 Changing the Basic Calculation	11
2.2 Sales Proceeds	11
2.3 Spouses and Civil Partners	12
2.4 Connected Persons	13
2.5 Connected Companies	13
2.6 Disposals not at 'Arm's Length'	14
2.7 Base Cost	14
2.8 Short Leases	16
2.9 Part Disposals of Shareholdings	17
2.10 Assets Subject to Holdover or Rollover Relief Claims	19
2.11 Assets Acquired Before 1st April 1982	20
2.12 Inherited Assets	21
Chapter 3 - What Happens Next?	22
3.1 The Story So Far	22
3.2 When Will the Increase Take Effect?	22
3.3 What Will the New Regime Be Like?	28
3.4 Which Businesses Will Be Exempted?	29
3.5 Property Businesses	32
3.6 What Reliefs Will Be Available?	33
3.7 Other Points to Consider	33
3.8 Summary	34
Chapter 4 - Should You Take Action Now?	36
4.1 Look Before You Leap	36
4.2 Knee-Jerk Reponses or Fatal Delays	36
4.3 Transaction Costs	37

4.4	Hidden Costs	38
4.5	Stock Market Investments	39
4.6	Property	39
4.7	Transfers versus Open Market Sales	40
4.8	Loss of Control	41
4.9	Loss of Income	41
4.10	Reduction in Capital	42
4.11	What If You Are Planning to Sell Up Anyway?	43

Chapter 5 - Creating a Capital Gain — 44

5.1	Why Do We Want to Create a Capital Gain?	44
5.2	The Four Main Ways to Create a Capital Gain	44
5.3	Transfers to Spouses	45

Chapter 6 - Open Market Sales — 47

6.1	Keeping it Simple	47
6.2	Repurchases and Replacements	47
6.3	Potential Savings	49
6.4	You May Have Longer Than You Think	50

Chapter 7 - Transfers to Another Individual — 51

7.1	Keeping it in the Family	51
7.2	Who Can You Transfer Assets To?	52
7.3	Potential Savings	53
7.4	Greater Savings	54
7.5	Business Assets and Holdover Relief	55
7.6	Partial Holdover Relief	58
7.7	Entrepreneurs' Relief	61
7.8	Jointly Held Property	64
7.9	Inheritance Tax	65
7.10	Transfers to Non-Resident Individuals	66

Chapter 8 - Transfers into Trust — 68

8.1	Keeping Control	68
8.2	Trusts and Holdover Relief	69
8.3	Trusts and Inheritance Tax	70
8.4	Avoiding Inheritance Tax	72
8.5	Trusts and Income Tax	73
8.6	Trusts and Capital Gains Tax	73
8.7	Trusts and Principal Private Residence Relief	74

Chapter 9 - Transfers to a Company — 75

9.1	Keeping it All	75
9.2	Incorporation	75
9.3	Capital Gains in Companies	76

9.4	Stamp Duty Land Tax on Transfers to Companies	78
9.5	Potential Savings	78
9.6	Profit Extraction Problems	80
9.7	Don't Give, Sell!	81
9.8	Obsolete Companies	82
9.9	Potential Savings with Holdover Relief	82
9.10	Potential Savings with Incorporation Relief	84

Chapter 10 - What If It Goes Wrong? — 86

10.1	Safety Nets	86
10.2	The Holdover Option	86
10.3	The Reinvestment Option	88
10.4	Re-Acquiring Shares	88
10.5	Creating Capital Losses	89

Chapter 11 - Other Planning Issues — 90

| 11.1 | Furnished holiday letting | 90 |
| 11.2 | Emigration | 91 |

Chapter 12 - Problem Areas — 94

12.1	Stamp Duty Land Tax	94
12.2	The Perils of Personal Use	95
12.3	Business Transfers	96
12.4	Transfers of Loss-Making Assets	96
12.5	Remittance Basis Drawbacks	96

Appendix A - Tax Rates and Allowances — 97

Appendix B - The European Union & The European Economic Area — 99

Appendix C - Connected Persons — 100

Appendix D - Indexation Relief Rates — 101

Appendix E - Short Leases — 103

Other Taxcafe Products & Services — 104

Disclaimer — 105

Introduction

The 18% flat rate of Capital Gains Tax introduced by the previous Government in 2008 is the lowest rate the tax has known since it was introduced by an earlier Labour Government under Harold Wilson almost half a century ago.

Within days of assuming office in May 2010, the new Conservative-Liberal Democrat coalition Government announced that it would be making radical changes to the Capital Gains Tax regime and would be increasing the rate of Capital Gains Tax to something 'at least close to Income Tax rates'.

Clearly, this means that major tax increases are in the pipeline. Anyone with prospective capital gains on a business, a property, investments, or any other assets may be exposed to Capital Gains Tax at a much higher rate.

Many people are considering their options and asking themselves key questions, such as:

- How will my business or investments be affected?
- Should I sell before the increase takes effect?
- When will that be?
- Is it already too late?
- Is it worth it?
- Is there another way I can beat the increase?

For the first five of these questions, my task in this guide is to give you as much information as possible to enable you to come to your own answers. I will look at some of the Government's options and consider which types of investments and businesses are likely to be subject to the biggest tax increases.

I will also look at the crucial question of when the increases may take place. No-one outside the Government actually knows the answer to this yet, but a detailed look at some of the factors involved will enable you to form your own view – an 'educated guess' if you like.

Another important area is the question of whether taking action to beat the Capital Gains Tax increase will actually be worth it in the end. To help you form an answer to this question, I will take a detailed look at some example scenarios and the potential outcomes under a new Capital Gains Tax regime. I will also consider some of the many practical issues which need to be taken into account in addition to the tax position.

I will then turn to the last and perhaps most important of those key questions: 'Is there another way I can beat the increase?' Or, to put it another way: 'Can I still beat the increase if I can't sell my business or investments before it takes effect, or I don't want to?'

Subject to a few provisos, the answer to these questions is an emphatic 'YES' and, in this guide, I will show you how.

I will explain how you can create a capital gain under the current regime at little or no tax cost and how this will enable you to make substantial overall savings when you eventually sell your business or investments.

I will guide you through each of the main methods available for creating a capital gain. More importantly, I will also provide a detailed guide to the other tax consequences arising, the further tax planning opportunities available, the pitfalls to watch out for and, where relevant, the new tax regime you will face after creating your gain.

In this time of great uncertainty, another question many people will be asking is 'What if it goes wrong? Or, in other words, can the tax planning be undone if it turns out that your capital gain is caught by the new regime after all?

There are no absolute guarantees here, as any new regime is bound to also include some new anti-avoidance rules but, based on current legislation, there are quite a few 'safety nets' available which should mean that you will have the opportunity to 'hedge your bets' and amend or undo your planning if it proves to be disadvantageous after all. Chapter 10 is devoted to an exploration of these possible escape routes.

Finally, we will wrap up the guide with a quick look at a couple of special planning issues and some important problem areas that you need to be aware of: as ever in tax planning, it is vital to take **all** taxes into account, not just the one that you are trying to avoid!

We may not yet know exactly what the future holds for Capital Gains Tax but, with the help of this guide, you can at least be prepared for it.

Scope of this Guide

This guide is aimed at all those who have a potential liability to UK Capital Gains Tax. Primarily, this will be UK resident or ordinarily resident individuals but non-UK residents may sometimes also be exposed to UK Capital Gains Tax.

This guide deals only with UK taxation issues. Foreign taxation is beyond its scope.

For tax purposes, the UK does not include the Channel Islands or the Isle of Man, but comprises only England, Scotland, Wales and Northern Ireland.

> **Wealth Warning**
>
> It is important to remember that both UK residents holding property, investments, or other assets located overseas and non-UK residents holding assets in the UK may also face foreign tax liabilities. Each country has its own tax system and income or gains which are exempt in the UK may nevertheless still be liable to tax elsewhere.
>
> Additionally, in some cases, citizens of another country who are resident in the UK for tax purposes may nevertheless still have obligations and liabilities under their own country's tax system. The USA, for example, imposes this type of obligation on its expatriate citizens.
>
> It is only when talking about taxpayers who are both UK residents and UK citizens, and who are investing exclusively in UK assets, that we can be absolutely certain that no other country has any right to tax the income or gains arising.

Finally, the reader must bear in mind the general nature of this guide. Individual circumstances vary and the tax implications of an individual's actions will vary with them. For this reason, it is always vital to get professional advice before undertaking any tax planning or other transactions which may have tax implications. The author cannot accept any responsibility for any loss which may arise as a consequence of any action taken, or any decision to refrain from action taken, as a result of reading this guide.

A Word about the Examples in this Guide

This guide is illustrated throughout by a number of examples.

Unless specifically stated to the contrary, all persons described in the examples in this guide are UK resident, ordinarily resident and domiciled for tax purposes.

In preparing the examples in this guide, it has been assumed that the UK tax regime will remain unchanged in the future except to the extent of any announcements already made at the time of publication and any further assumptions regarding changes to the Capital Gains Tax regime which are set out in the text.

Nevertheless, if there is one thing which we can predict with any certainty it is the fact that change **will** occur. The reader must bear this in mind when reviewing the results of our examples.

All persons described in the examples in this guide are entirely fictional characters created specifically for the purposes of this guide. Any similarities to actual persons, living or dead, or to fictional characters created by any other author, are entirely coincidental.

Chapter 1

The 'Current' Capital Gains Tax Regime

1.1 OVERVIEW

Before we can begin to look at the potential impact of the forthcoming changes to the Capital Gains Tax regime, we need to have a brief look at the current regime. After all, we cannot work out how much extra tax we might face if we don't know how much we already face at the moment.

When I say the 'current' regime, I am referring to the Capital Gains Tax regime which currently sits on the statute books. Whether it actually still applies to capital gains arising today is another question and we will look at this in Chapter 3. For the rest of this chapter and the next though, I will assume that it does currently still apply.

1.2 THE FLAT RATE REGIME

Since 6th April 2008, the UK has had a simple, flat rate, regime for Capital Gains Tax.

Subject to a few exemptions and reliefs, Capital Gains Tax is charged at a single flat rate of 18%. All individuals and trusts pay the same rate, regardless of the level of their income. A billionaire selling off a multi-million pound investment portfolio pays 18%; a basic rate taxpayer selling a single investment property which they've owned for 20 years pays 18%.

In the absence of any applicable exemptions, reliefs, or other relevant adjustments, the basic Capital Gains Tax calculation simply consists of taking the sales proceeds received, deducting your purchase cost, and multiplying the answer by 18%.

Example

In 1990, Hilary bought some shares in Tensing plc for £10,000. In May 2010, she sells them for £110,000. She therefore has a taxable gain of £100,000 and a Capital Gains Tax bill of £18,000.

This very simple calculation can be expressed as: **'Proceeds minus Cost times 18%'** and it lies at the heart of every Capital Gains Tax computation.

In practice, however, the Capital Gains Tax charge is often reduced by various exemptions and reliefs. We will take a brief look at some of the main exemptions and reliefs currently available in Section 1.5.

1.3 WHO PAYS CAPITAL GAINS TAX?

Capital Gains Tax is payable by UK resident or ordinarily resident individuals and trusts on the capital gains arising on disposal of assets situated anywhere in the world.

Companies do not usually pay Capital Gains Tax: they are subject to Corporation Tax on their capital gains. This gives rise to some major planning opportunities, as we shall see later in Chapter 9.

Non-UK residents are not usually subject to UK Capital Gains Tax unless they are:

- a) Ordinarily resident in the UK, or
- b) Operating a business in the UK (including such businesses operated through a branch or agency).

In the latter case, the non-UK resident is subject to UK Capital Gains Tax on the assets employed in their UK business. This does not generally apply to investment properties owned by non-UK residents, including furnished holiday lets.

UK resident individuals who are either non-UK ordinarily resident or non-UK domiciled may claim the remittance basis of taxation. This means that they may elect to only pay UK Capital Gains Tax on capital gains arising overseas if and when they remit the sales proceeds to the UK. There are, however, some potential drawbacks to the remittance basis which we will look at later in Section 12.5.

The concepts of residence, ordinary residence and domicile can be quite complex and, in doubtful cases, it will be necessary to obtain professional advice to determine where you stand. Briefly, however, and as a rough guide only, they can be described as follows:

Residence: The country where you live now.
Ordinary Residence: The country where you usually live.
Domicile: Your permanent, long-term home (often, but not always, your country of birth).

1.4 WHEN IS CAPITAL GAINS TAX PAYABLE?

Capital Gains Tax falls under the self-assessment system and is payable by reference to UK tax years.

The UK tax year runs from 6th April in one calendar year to 5th April in the next. Hence, for example, the year ending 5th April 2011 is the UK tax year 2010/11.

The Capital Gains Tax payable for each tax year is due for payment by 31st January following that tax year. Hence, for example, the Capital Gains Tax on a capital gain arising during the year ending 5th April 2011 is due for payment by 31st January 2012.

Capital Gains Tax is payable in a single lump sum. The payments on account system which applies to Income Tax payable under self-assessment does not apply to Capital Gains Tax.

For those claiming the remittance basis on capital gains arising overseas (see Section 1.3), Capital Gains Tax is payable by 31st January following the end of the UK tax year in which sales proceeds are remitted to the UK.

1.5 EXEMPTIONS AND RELIEFS

Whilst there is currently only one single rate of Capital Gains Tax, the effective rate paid in many cases is reduced due to the operation of various exemptions and reliefs. The main items to be aware of may briefly be described as follows:

The Annual Exemption: Currently £10,100, this exempts the first part of each individual's capital gains in each tax year. The exemption for trusts is generally £5,050.

Principal Private Residence Relief: Exempts the capital gain arising on your own home. Partial relief is available when the property has been your main residence only part of the time.

Private Letting Relief: Extends (up to double) the partial relief available on a property which has been your main residence at some time during your ownership but which has also been rented out. The additional relief provided is subject to a maximum of £40,000 per property per person.

Entrepreneurs' Relief: Exempts four ninths of the capital gains on qualifying business assets. This produces an effective Capital Gains Tax rate of 10% on such gains (18% of five ninths is the same as 10% of the whole). Generally requires the disposal or cessation of a business or the disposal of an interest in a business. Applies to disposals taking place after 5th April 2008 and is subject to a lifetime limit of £2m of capital gains per person (of which only a maximum of £1m can apply to gains arising before 6th April 2010).

Holdover Relief: Can be used to exempt or reduce the capital gain on gifts, or sales at below market value, of qualifying business assets, or on asset transfers chargeable to Inheritance Tax. Gains held over reduce the recipient's allowable cost for the asset, so this is a deferral rather than an absolute relief.

Rollover Relief: Another form of deferral. Capital gains on the disposal of qualifying business assets can be deferred by reinvesting the sales proceeds in new qualifying business assets.

Incorporation Relief: Can be used to exempt the capital gain arising on the transfer of a qualifying business to a company. This is effectively a variation of holdover relief. In this case, the held over gain reduces the transferor's allowable cost for their company shares rather than the company's allowable cost for the transferred assets.

Loss Relief: Capital losses are automatically set off against any capital gains arising in the same tax year. Any excess is carried forward and set off against capital gains arising in future tax years but only to the extent necessary to reduce the total gains in those years to the amount of the annual exemption.

Capital losses are personal: they cannot be transferred to any other person and they are extinguished on death.

Note
The definition of 'qualifying business assets' differs from one relief to another.

Chapter 2

Special Cases

2.1 CHANGING THE BASIC CALCULATION

In some cases, the simple calculation described in Section 1.2 needs to be amended. This can arise in a number of ways and often involves substituting a different figure for either cost or sales proceeds, or even both.

These amendments arise due to a combination of tax reliefs and anti-avoidance measures and we will look at all the major issues to be aware of in this chapter.

The most important aspect of the special cases which we are going to look at in this chapter, however, is the fact that the amendments to the figure we need to use for sales proceeds will often give us the opportunity to create a capital gain: thus enabling us to 'cash in' our gains under the current low tax regime.

This is particularly gratifying since it means that we will be performing one of my favourite tricks: using the Government's own anti-avoidance legislation for our benefit!

2.2 SALES PROCEEDS

The sales proceeds figure to be used in a Capital Gains Tax computation would normally be the actual sales price of the asset less any incidental disposal costs, such as legal fees, the cost of advertising the asset for sale, or stockbroker's dealing charges.

In some cases, however, a different figure must be used: which we often term the 'deemed sales proceeds'. This applies in the case of:

- Transfers to spouses or civil partners (see Section 2.3)
- Transfers to connected persons (see Section 2.4)
- Disposals not made at 'arm's length' (see Section 2.6)

The deemed sales proceeds arising in some of these situations lies at the heart of much of the planning in this guide.

2.3 SPOUSES AND CIVIL PARTNERS

One of the odd things about being in the position of trying to create capital gains is that tax reliefs which are normally beneficial can become a hindrance. This is very well illustrated by the case of transfers of assets to spouses or civil partners.

A transfer to your spouse or civil partner is exempt from Capital Gains Tax. This is achieved by treating the transfer as a 'no gain no loss' transfer. In other words, the deemed sales proceeds is the sum which ensures that the transferor has neither a capital gain nor a capital loss. The actual amount paid by the transferee, if any, is ignored for Capital Gains Tax purposes (but may still be relevant for other taxes, including Stamp Duty or Stamp Duty Land Tax).

Under the current Capital Gains Tax regime, this generally means that the asset is deemed to have been sold for a sum equivalent to the transferor's cost.

Whilst, in other circumstances, this 'spouse exemption' can be extremely useful, it means that a transfer to your spouse or civil partner cannot be used to create a capital gain.

The exemption for transfers between spouses or civil partners starts on the date of marriage (or registration of the civil partnership) and ends at the end of the tax year in which the couple permanently separate (or on the date of a decree absolute finalising divorce proceedings if this is earlier).

Note: Unlike several other countries, the UK has refused to adopt the term 'marriage' for a registered civil partnership. In UK tax law, however, the effect is exactly the same. To save a little space, therefore, I will simply use the term 'spouse' to denote both spouses and civil partners throughout the rest of this guide.

Please also note, however, that the term 'spouse' only covers legally married husbands and wives and registered civil partners and does not cover unmarried partners of any description.

2.4 CONNECTED PERSONS

For tax purposes, each of us is deemed to be 'connected' to certain other people including our children, our parents and our siblings. A more comprehensive list is set out in Appendix C.

Any transfer of an asset to a connected person other than your spouse is treated for Capital Gains Tax purposes as if it were a sale of that asset for its open market value.

Under the right circumstances, this can provide just the opportunity we need to create capital gains now, which can be taxed under the current low Capital Gains Tax regime. We will look at the practical application of this, and the savings it may generate, in Chapter 7.

As explained in Section 2.3, a transfer to your spouse which is covered by the 'spouse exemption' will not produce the same result.

It may be worth noting, however, that a separated spouse remains a connected person right up until the granting of a decree absolute. Hence, a transfer to your estranged spouse after the end of the tax year in which you separated would create a capital gain in the same way as a transfer to any other connected person.

2.5 CONNECTED COMPANIES

As you will see from Appendix C, one of the 'connected persons', to which a transfer must be treated as a sale at market value, is a company under your own control (or controlled by your spouse or relatives).

This provides an additional opportunity to create capital gains to be taxed under the current low Capital Gains Tax regime.

However, in some cases, a transfer to a company can go even further than this. Where qualifying business assets are transferred into a company, it can be possible to avoid Capital Gains Tax altogether. This is something which we will explore further in Chapter 7 but, at this stage, it is worth knowing that this possibility may exist.

2.6 DISPOSALS NOT AT 'ARM'S LENGTH'

As explained in Section 2.4, any transfer to a connected person (other than your spouse) is deemed to take place at open market value.

The same treatment also applies to other transfers which are not made at 'arm's length'. This, for example, could apply where the transaction is part of a larger transaction or part of a series of transactions.

Perhaps more usefully, it could also apply where, although not officially classed as 'connected', there is nevertheless a special relationship between the transferor and transferee, such that they are not likely to transact with each other at 'arm's length'. The best example of this type of 'special relationship' is probably unmarried partners, including future spouses where the transfer takes place before the date of marriage or registration of a civil partnership.

In short, therefore, a transfer of an asset to an unmarried partner can be used to create a capital gain in the same way as a transfer to a connected person.

Couples planning to marry or enter a civil partnership in future can also create a capital gain by transferring assets beforehand.

2.7 BASE COST

The eligible cost of an asset for Capital Gains Tax purposes is generally referred to as the 'base cost'. In most cases, this is simply the actual purchase price of the asset plus other incidental purchase costs, such as Stamp Duty, Stamp Duty Land Tax or legal fees. Improvement or enhancement costs may also be added, such as the cost of an extension built on a property, or the cost of additional shares acquired under a rights issue.

As with sales proceeds, however, there are some special cases where the base cost will be something different and will not be based on actual purchase price. This is important because, when we move on to look at the consequences of creating capital gains in later chapters, it will be essential to know what your base cost is.

Furthermore, any planning which involves creating a capital gain will generally only be worthwhile where it produces a greater base cost for the transferee. Hence, again, we need to understand what that base cost will be.

The main instances where the base cost of an asset for Capital Gains Tax purposes will be something other than its purchase price include:

- Assets acquired from your spouse
- Assets acquired from a connected person
- Assets acquired by way of a transaction not made at 'arm's length'
- Short leases (see Section 2.8)
- Shares where not all of the holding is being disposed of at the same time (see Section 2.9)
- Assets which have previously been subject to a holdover or rollover relief claim (see Section 2.10)
- Assets acquired before 1st April 1982 (see Section 2.11)
- Inherited assets (see Section 2.12)

The base cost of an asset acquired under any of the first three headings above will be the same as the transferor's deemed sales proceeds, as detailed in Sections 2.3, 2.4 and 2.6.

In the case of assets acquired from a connected person other than your spouse, and other assets acquired by way of a transaction not made at 'arm's length', this will generally be the asset's open market value at the time of acquisition: thus providing the greater base cost which is required for much of the planning we will see later on.

In the case of an asset acquired from your spouse before 6th April 2008 and which they had originally acquired before 1st April 1998, your base cost will include the indexation relief which your spouse would have been entitled to if they had sold the asset.

The rates of indexation relief applying in the case of an asset transferred from your spouse to you at any time between 1st April 1998 and 5th April 2008 are set out in Appendix D.

Example

Tom bought a buy-to-let property for £50,000 in September 1986. In March 2008, he transferred the property to his wife Romana.

If Tom had sold his property at that time, he would have been entitled to indexation relief of 65.4% (see Appendix D), or £32,700. This is therefore added to Romana's base cost for the property, making this £82,700.

Note that indexation cannot create a capital loss so, in the unlikely event that Romana were to sell the property for between £50,000 and £82,700, she would be treated as having no gain and no loss. Only if she sold the property for less than £50,000 would she have a capital loss and, even then, it would be restricted to the difference between Tom's original purchase cost and her sale proceeds.

2.8 SHORT LEASES

A short lease with less than 50 years remaining at the time of disposal is treated as a 'wasting asset'. Anyone who assigns such a lease is required to reduce their base cost in accordance with the schedule set out in Appendix E.

For example, for a lease with 20 years remaining, and which had more than 50 years remaining when first acquired, the base cost must be reduced to 72.77% of the original amount.

Where the lease had less than 50 years remaining when originally acquired, the necessary reduction in base cost is achieved by multiplying the original cost by the factor applying at the time of sale and dividing by the factor applying at the time of purchase.

Example

John takes out a ten year lease over a building and pays a premium of £10,000. Five years later, John assigns his lease to Roy at a premium of £6,000.

When calculating his capital gain, the amount which John may claim as his base cost is £10,000 x 26.722/46.695 = £5,723.

Note that the **grant** of a short lease of less than 50 years' duration (out of a freehold title or a superior lease) is treated quite differently. For further details see the Taxcafe.co.uk guide *'How to Avoid Property Tax'*.

2.9 PART DISPOSALS OF SHAREHOLDINGS

Where a person owns shares in any company which they have acquired piecemeal, in more than one batch (or, to be more precise, at more than one price), a system of averaging is generally used to determine the base cost when the shares are sold or transferred. This, of course, is only relevant when the person is disposing of only part of their shareholding.

Subject to a few exceptions (which we will look at later in this section), the system works by pooling together all of the shares:

- of the same class,
- in the same company,
- held by the same person,
- in the same capacity.

The last point means that shares held in a different capacity are not pooled together. This, for example, might mean shares held as a bare trustee on behalf of a minor child, or as a nominee on behalf of an investment club.

Similarly, shares held through an Individual Savings Account ('ISA') are not pooled with other shares.

In official terminology, the pool of shares is known as the 'Section 104 Holding'.

It is very important to understand the pooling system because it means that a disposal of shares may have a different result to what you might otherwise have expected. This, in turn, will be critical when undertaking any of the planning which we are going to look at later in the guide.

Example

In 1999, Sarah bought 10,000 shares in Sidrat plc at £1.20 per share. Later, in 2007, she bought a further 5,000 shares at £2.25 per share.

Her Section 104 Holding is made up as follows:

	No.	£
Purchased in 1999 @ £1.20	10,000	£12,000
Purchased in 2007 @ £2.25	5,000	£11,250
Section 104 Holding	15,000	£23,250

In June 2010, Sarah sells 5,000 shares at a price of £4.25 per share, realising proceeds of £21,250.

Sarah mistakenly believes that she will be treated as having sold the shares she bought in 2007, so that she will have made a gain of £2 per share, totalling £10,000, which will be covered by her annual exemption.

Sadly, Sarah is wrong. Instead, she is treated as having sold 5,000 shares out of her Section 104 Holding of 15,000. Her base cost is therefore just £7,750 (£23,250 x 5,000/15,000), giving her a capital gain of £13,500 (£21,250 - £7,750).

Exceptions

Shares issued to a person as an employee of the issuing company must be pooled separately, as must any shares where the holder's rights to dispose of those shares is subject to restrictions (e.g. under the terms of a shareholders' agreement).

Where shares are bought and sold on the same day, the disposals are first matched with the new shares before the Section 104 Holding.

Similarly, where any shares of the same class are re-acquired within the next 30 days after the date of a disposal, the disposals are matched with these before the Section 104 Holding (but after any shares acquired on the day of the disposal).

Example Continued

After her sale in June 2010, Sarah has a Section 104 Holding of 10,000 shares with a base cost of £15,500 (£23,250 - £7,750 or £23,250 x 10,000/15,000).

On 1st September 2010, she buys a further 1,000 shares at £5 each then sells 6,000 shares for £5.50 each. On 30th September 2010, she buys 2,000 shares for £2.75 each.

Her capital gain arising on 1st September 2010 is calculated as follows:

	£	£
Sale proceeds – 6,000 @ £5.50		33,000
Less Base Cost:		
1,000 shares acquired same day @ £5	5,000	
2,000 shares acquired within 30 days thereafter @ £2.75	5,500	
3,000 shares from Section 104 Holding £15,500 x 3,000/10,000	4,650	
Total Base Cost		15,150
Capital Gain		17,850

Again, Sarah has a different capital gain to what she might have expected: few investors would expect to need to match subsequent purchases with their disposals if they had not previously been advised of this rule!

The '30 day rule' is an anti-avoidance measure designed to prevent 'Bread and Breakfasting', but it can actually be used to your advantage in some cases, as we shall see in Section 10.4.

2.10 ASSETS SUBJECT TO HOLDOVER OR ROLLOVER RELIEF CLAIMS

As explained in Section 1.5, it is sometimes possible to defer the capital gain on the disposal of an asset by claiming to 'hold over' that gain.

However, as a consequence of any such 'holdover claim' made when an asset was acquired, the base cost of that asset will be reduced by the amount of the held over gain.

This could apply in the case of an asset received by way of a gift or a purchase at below market value which:

- Is a qualifying business asset (see Section 7.5)
- Gave rise to a chargeable lifetime transfer for Inheritance Tax purposes when it was received (see Section 8.3), or
- Was received between 6th April 1980 and 13th March 1989.

We will take a more detailed look at the effect of hold over relief claims in Chapter 7.

Rollover Relief

The base cost of an asset will also be reduced where a previous capital gain was deferred by reinvesting some or all of the sale proceeds in it.

This applies most commonly to business premises, such as shops or offices, but can also apply to other business assets including goodwill, various agricultural quotas, ships, aircraft and even satellites!

2.11 ASSETS ACQUIRED BEFORE 1ST APRIL 1982

The base cost of any asset acquired before 1st April 1982 is its open market value on 31st March 1982.

Any purchase cost, incidental acquisition costs, improvement or enhancement expenditure incurred before 1st April 1982 is ignored. We must simply take the open market value of the asset on 31st March 1982 in place of all these costs.

Where further qualifying improvement or enhancement expenditure is incurred after 31st March 1982, however, this may be added to the asset's base cost in the usual way.

Where further shares of the same class in the same company are acquired after 31st March 1982, the shares are pooled together as a single 'Section 104 Holding' in the manner described in Section 2.9. For this purpose, the actual cost of the shares acquired after 31st March 1982 is simply added to the market value of the shares already held on that date.

2.12 INHERITED ASSETS

Transfers of assets arising on death are exempt from Capital Gains Tax. The recipient is treated as having acquired the asset for its open market value at the date of the deceased's death. This is often referred to as the Capital Gains Tax 'uplift on death' and it gives rise to that same increase in base cost which we have talked about in other cases.

The 'uplift on death' applies equally whether the asset has passed to the new owner under the terms of the deceased's Will, by survivorship, or under the laws of intestacy and, in all of these cases, it does not matter when legal title actually passes: it is the market value at date of death which becomes the new owner's base cost.

This rule takes precedence over the rules for lifetime transfers of assets to spouses (see Section 2.3), so the 'uplift on death' still applies where a widow, widower or surviving civil partner inherits assets from their spouse. This gives rise to some deathbed Capital Gains Tax planning opportunities which are examined in the Taxcafe.co.uk guide *'How to Avoid Inheritance Tax'*.

A purchase of assets from the deceased's estate is not the same as inheriting that asset and the normal rules set out elsewhere in this chapter will apply to determine the new owner's base cost. Such purchases often arise as a result of Inheritance Tax planning measures.

Taking Capital Gains Tax in isolation, we can see that a good way to avoid Capital Gains Tax is to simply retain your assets until you die. The problem, however, is that most assets are subject to Inheritance Tax on your death, so this strategy should generally only be considered if you also have a means to avoid Inheritance Tax as well.

It is, however, possible to identify a few areas where retaining assets until death is an effective way to avoid Capital Gains Tax without giving rise to additional Inheritance Tax liabilities. For a detailed examination of this subject, see the Taxcafe.co.uk guide *'How to Avoid Inheritance Tax'*.

Chapter 3

What Happens Next?

3.1 THE STORY SO FAR

In the first two chapters, we have looked at the existing Capital Gains Tax regime before any changes are made by the new coalition Government. We have teased out a few planning ideas already but all of this is, of course, subject to what comes out in the emergency Budget on 22nd June 2010.

So far, we only have the following statement, taken from the coalition's 'programme for government', to go on:

> *"We will seek ways of taxing non-business capital gains at rates similar or close to those applied to income, with generous exemptions for entrepreneurial business activities."*

In this chapter, I am going to take a detailed look at what this statement may mean and what impact it will have on business owners, property investors, stock market investors and others with assets exposed to Capital Gains Tax, such as second homes.

I will not always be able to come to a firm conclusion, but I will give you a better idea of some of the probabilities.

Let's start by considering when the new Capital Gains Tax regime is likely to take effect.

3.2 WHEN WILL THE INCREASE TAKE EFFECT?

In this section, I am going to consider the possible dates on which the coalition Government's new Capital Gains Tax regime might take effect. It is important to stress, however, that no-one outside the Government actually knows the answer to this!

The potential candidates for the date of the change include:

- Backdating to 6th April 2010
- Immediately on Budget Day: 22nd June 2010
- A later date during the current tax year, such as 6th October 2010 or 1st January 2011
- Next year: 6th April 2011
- The year after: 6th April 2012
- Never

Let's look at each of these in turn.

Backdating to 6th April 2010

From the Government's point of view, backdating the Capital Gains Tax increase to the beginning of the current tax year has the following advantages:

- It's simple to administer with none of the problems created by changing the regime in the middle of a tax year.
- It raises badly needed revenue to help reduce the deficit as soon as possible.
- It prevents anyone from being able to beat the increase by taking the kind of measures which we will be discussing later in this guide.

The last point is, of course, a serious concern and we will address this in Chapter 10 when we look at some of the possible 'safety nets'.

As we can see, from the Government's point of view, a backdating of the increase to 6th April 2010 has a lot of merit. However, a backdated increase also carries some serious problems.

Firstly, there is the fact that this amounts to retrospective taxation. Fundamentally, under European Law, this is contrary to citizens' basic human rights. The Government would therefore need to justify this measure to the European Union or else face the prospect of having its new tax regime outlawed by the European Court of Justice. I cannot see either of these appealing to Messrs Cameron and Clegg.

However, the Government may be able to rely on an 'escape clause' within European Law. This basically says that, whilst retrospective taxation should generally be avoided, it could be justified in cases where a member state faces an urgent need to raise additional funds as a matter of national emergency.

There is therefore a potential argument that the UK deficit is so severe that retrospective taxation is justified in this case.

The second problem facing the coalition, however, is that a backdating of the Capital Gains Tax increase would be deeply unpopular with many important and influential sectors of the UK electorate, especially within the business community and amongst retired taxpayers reliant on investments for their income.

I have even heard some people say: 'It's just not Tory behaviour'. Well, we'll see on 22nd June.

Verdict: A backdated increase is possible but my personal opinion is that it is unlikely.

Immediately on Budget Day (22nd June)

Increasing Capital Gains Tax on Budget Day would avoid the spectre of 'retrospective taxation' which, I suspect, the new Government would find very hard to shake off.

An immediate increase could still cause problems under European Law, as this also gives citizens the right to reasonable warning of forthcoming increases. Then again, we have been warned, haven't we, so this may not be an insurmountable problem for the Government.

The bigger problem with an immediate increase is that it would cause massive administrative problems. The current tax year would have to be divided into two different periods for Capital Gains Tax purposes. This would be very difficult for HM Revenue and Customs to administer and would involve a major re-write of the software for the self-assessment system. The costs involved would be significant and could perhaps be hard to justify when the Government has pledged to make £6Bn worth of savings in the next ten months.

These problems would not be quite so bad if the Government were proposing a simple increase in the Capital Gains Tax rate. However, the proposal seems more like a return to the pre-2008 system of taxing each individual on capital gains at their marginal Income Tax rate, with a system of further reliefs for business assets. Adopting such a comprehensive regime change in the middle of the tax year would be a complete nightmare for all concerned.

However, the Government has stressed again and again that reducing the deficit is its most urgent priority. With this in mind, they may perceive that an immediate increase has the benefit of raising more revenue in the short term than a delayed increase and has the further merit of preventing a prolonged period during which taxpayers are all able to plan to avoid that increase.

Verdict: There is a significant possibility of an immediate increase on 22nd June. However, the practical difficulties for HM Revenue and Customs and the Government may be too great to justify such a move.

Later in the Current Tax Year

Are there secret talks going on in Brussels to establish just how soon the Government can implement a Capital Gains Tax increase without ruffling any feathers under European Law?

What about HM Revenue and Customs? Is there a mid-year date which might suit them better than 22nd June: something more logical, like half-way through the tax year on 6th October, or at the start of the new calendar year on 1st January 2011?

Any mid-year increase still carries administrative problems but a later date may be more justifiable to the European Union and the UK electorate.

There is plenty of precedent for mid-year changes. Only last year, the ISA allowances were increased for people aged over 50 with effect from 6th October.

A date later in the current tax year still ensures an early start to revenue-raising from this measure and does reduce the window of opportunity for the tax planning designed to avoid the increase.

As a real outsider, the Government could even seize the opportunity to change the UK tax year to a calendar year in order to align us with most of the rest of the G7 and the European Union. They could then bring in the new Capital Gains Tax regime on 1st January 2011, at the start of our first new-style tax year. (Cameron and Clegg aligning with the USA and the EU? OK, probably not!)

Verdict: An increase later in the current tax year is a possibility but my personal opinion is that it has a fairly low probability.

Next Year (6th April 2011)

Changing the Capital Gains Tax regime from 6th April 2011 at the beginning of the next tax year would be far simpler to administer than any mid-year change.

Deferring the change until then also avoids any European Law issues and allows for a reasonable period of consultation with key sectors of the electorate, thus reducing the political damage for the coalition parties.

The main disadvantages from the Government's point of view are that:

- The revenue-raising from this measure would be delayed.
- There would be a lengthy window of opportunity for taxpayers to plan to avoid the increase.

On the first point, it is worth mentioning that the Capital Gains Tax increase is being used to pay for the planned increase in the Income Tax personal allowance. This itself is not due to take place until 6th April 2011 so, logically, it would seem to make sense that the Capital Gains Tax increase takes place on the same date.

Still, when did logic ever come into tax? Furthermore, in Government cashflow terms, an increase in the Capital Gains Tax rate on 6th April 2011 would not start to bring in any extra Capital Gains Tax until January 2013, whereas the increase in the Income Tax personal allowance will have an almost immediate impact on the PAYE tax collected by the Government.

But there's another way to look at all this which I, for one, hope the Government realises.

If the Government announces that the increase will take place from 6th April 2011, it will give taxpayers plenty of time to plan to avoid the increase. Much of that planning (as we shall see later in the guide) will involve triggering capital gains to be taxed at the current low rate of 18%.

Many of the assets subject to this planning might not have been disposed of for many years. In other words, the planning designed to beat the Capital Gains Tax increase would yield a significantly larger amount of Capital Gains Tax this year under the current regime than would otherwise have been the case.

As a result, the Government would receive significant additional revenue in January 2012, twelve months earlier than when it will actually start to receive any extra tax from the increased rate itself. Such additional revenue may also be considerably greater than would have been generated by a back-dated or immediate tax increase.

At the same time, taxpayers will feel they have been treated more fairly by being given adequate warning of the increase and satisfied that they have taken the necessary steps to avoid it.

It looks like a win-win situation to me!

Verdict: My personal opinion is that an increase from 6th April 2011 seems to be the most likely outcome, especially if the Government can see the potential cashflow benefit of allowing taxpayers to pay extra tax at 18% this year!

The Year After (6th April 2012)

The statement in Section 3.1 starts with the phrase "We will seek ways of taxing...." To me, this suggests that they don't really have a clue exactly how they're going to do it. If so, it may take a little longer to work out the right method and this could potentially delay the increase until 6th April 2012.

Having said that, however, they do have plenty of time to get their act together before 6th April 2011 and the deficit demands that action is taken sooner rather than later.

Verdict: Any further delay in the increase beyond 6th April 2011 seems unlikely.

Never

As I said earlier, some people are saying the Capital Gains Tax increase is 'just not Tory behaviour' and there is a fair amount of grumbling from Conservative backbenchers and supporters.

Maintaining the support of these people will be crucial to the coalition, so it is just possible that we could see the Capital Gains Tax increase first delayed and then shelved in favour of other, more effective, measures.

More likely, however, as so often in politics, we may see some sort of compromise deal with a slight watering down of the current proposals rather than seeing them shelved altogether.

Verdict: Anything is possible, but a complete 'U-Turn' on the Capital Gains Tax increase seems extremely unlikely.

3.3 WHAT WILL THE NEW REGIME BE LIKE?

According to the statement in Section 3.1, the coalition Government intends to tax individuals on their capital gains at "rates similar or close to those applied to income".

Note the use of the word 'rates' in the plural: this suggests more than one rate and could signal a return to a system where each individual pays Capital Gains Tax at a rate determined by their top rate of Income Tax.

However, the phrase 'similar or close to' also suggests that the new regime will not necessarily involve paying Capital Gains Tax at exactly the same rate as Income Tax. This could mean many things, including a possible cap at 40%. We know the Conservatives would like to abolish the new 50% rate of Income Tax, but that the deficit prevents them from making it a priority at the moment. They may at least be able to afford to keep the 'super tax' rate from applying to capital gains however.

The 'similar or close to' phrase could also mean that there will be some reduction in the rate for longer-term gains: perhaps a reinstatement of indexation relief (which still applies to capital gains made by companies under Corporation Tax), or some new type of taper relief. It could even simply mean that capital gains will be taxed at some proportion of the applicable Income Tax rate, such as three quarters, making the rate 30% for a higher rate taxpayer, but just 15% for a basic rate taxpayer.

There are too many variables for us to form a clear picture of what the new regime will be like, but it is possible that higher rate taxpayers will suffer Capital Gains Tax at rates of at least 30% or 40% subject to any reliefs which are available for long-term gains and for those 'entrepreneurial business activities'.

3.4 WHICH BUSINESSES WILL BE EXEMPTED?

The most welcome part of the statement in Section 3.1 must be the final phrase: "with generous exemptions for entrepreneurial business activities".

The problem is that we do not have any definition of what the new Government thinks constitutes an 'entrepreneurial business activity' and nor do we know how generous these exemptions will be.

Up until now, the UK tax system has generally only given favoured tax status to three types of business:

- Trading activities
- Professions
- Furnished holiday letting

'Trading activities' covers a very broad range of businesses, including trades as diverse as manufacturing, retail and property development, but it specifically excludes any form of property rental business or any investment activity, such as investing in stocks and shares.

Professions include lawyers, doctors and accountants. Whilst technically not a 'trade', these activities are treated in almost the same way throughout most of the UK tax system.

Furnished holiday letting has had a special tax regime all of its own since 1984 and this has meant that properties employed in this type of business have been eligible for all of the same Capital Gains Tax reliefs as trading properties. For details of the qualifying conditions for furnished holiday lets see Section 11.1. For further information on the current furnished holiday letting tax regime see the Taxcafe.co.uk guides *'How to Avoid Property Tax'* or *'Furnished Holiday Lets: Emergency Tax Planning Guide'*.

The furnished holiday letting regime was expanded to properties throughout the European Economic Area (see Appendix B) in 2009 (with retrospective effect) but was due for abolition on 6th April 2010 under proposals announced by the previous Government.

The regime was saved by a last minute reprieve before the general election. That reprieve was spearheaded by Messrs Cameron and Clegg, so there is every reason to suppose that they will look sympathetically on furnished holiday letting landlords within their new Capital Gains Tax regime.

What the coalition are actually saying on the subject is:

> "We will take measures to fulfil our EU treaty obligations in regard to the taxation of holiday letting that do not penalise UK-based businesses."

The background to this statement is the fact that the previous Government was forced to expand the furnished holiday letting regime to the rest of the European Economic Area under European Law. This, they felt, made the regime too generous so they simply decided to abolish the whole thing.

The new Government seems to be suggesting that they will find a way to preserve the regime without allowing it to be over-generous to owners of foreign holiday homes: the big fear the Labour Government seemed to have. (This would never have happened if HM Revenue and Customs had simply enforced the current regime's qualifying conditions properly.)

My suspicion is that the furnished holiday letting regime will survive but some of the qualifying conditions will be tightened, not so that properties outside the UK are specifically excluded (that would be contrary to European Law) but so that, in practice, it would become unlikely that many such properties would qualify.

Trades and Professions

Are all trades and professions automatically certain of being regarded as 'entrepreneurial business activities'?

We cannot be certain on this point. There is no guarantee that, just because an activity is a trade or profession under general law, then it must necessarily qualify as 'entrepreneurial'.

Certain activities are indeed excluded from qualifying for some existing tax reliefs. These exclusions generally seem to focus on:

- Professions (e.g. accountant and lawyers)
- Land or property-based trades (e.g. property developers, hotels and nursing homes)
- Agricultural activities (e.g. farming and market gardening)
- Dealing in any form of investments (including property)
- Financial services (e.g. banking and insurance)

Conceivably, therefore, and whilst it may seem grossly unfair, some or all of these activities could be excluded from those 'generous exemptions'.

Ownership Criteria

As with previous Capital Gains Tax regimes, it may also be the way in which businesses are owned which determines whether they are 'entrepreneurial'. We may therefore see tests to determine how much the owner is involved in the business and potential exclusions for quoted shares.

In Conclusion

There are a range of possible outcomes here.

At the most optimistic end of the scale, the exemptions under the new regime may be available to all trades and professions, as well as a new and more restricted form of furnished holiday letting.

At the pessimistic end, the exemptions may only cover trading activities and may even be subject to additional exclusions.

3.5 PROPERTY BUSINESSES

Apart from furnished holiday letting (see Sections 3.4 and 11.1), the Capital Gains Tax regime has seldom given any favourable treatment to property rental businesses.

Successive Governments, the Courts and HM Revenue and Customs all seem to have regarded property rental as a passive investment activity. Whilst many of us know this to be far from the truth, it has nevertheless left us with a tax system where rental properties are often fully exposed to Capital Gains Tax.

This attitude may also be at least partly responsible for the consistent under-supply of residential accommodation in the UK.

Is there any hope that the new Government will 'see the light', accept that property rental businesses are an entrepreneurial activity, and provide them with appropriate exemptions under the new Capital Gains Tax regime?

If there is any hope, it must lie in the hands of representative bodies like the British Property Federation, the National Landlords Association and the Scottish Association of Landlords. If these bodies can lobby the Government effectively enough, a change of attitude may be achieved and the appropriate exemptions could be won.

In the meantime, however, many landlords and their advisers are planning for the worst and assuming that, as usual, any exemptions will not be coming their way.

3.6 WHAT RELIEFS WILL BE AVAILABLE?

We have no idea exactly what form the 'generous exemptions' described in the statement in Section 3.1 will take.

It is interesting that the Government has chosen the word 'exemption' rather than 'relief'. To me, an 'exemption' suggests complete exemption from tax, whereas 'relief' would imply a reduced rate or deferral. Before we get too excited though, we have to consider that they may actually mean an 'exemption' from any increase or, in other words, the retention of the existing effective rate of 10% under entrepreneurs' relief, or 18% in other cases.

Conceivably, therefore, qualifying business assets may continue to be subject to the same effective rate of 10% which applies in a limited number of cases under the current regime and which also applied in many more cases under the pre-2008 regime.

Alternatively, we may see some other reduced rate applying, such as half of the main rate, for example. This might then give higher rate taxpayers an effective Capital Gains Tax rate of 20% on disposals of qualifying business assets.

Anything less than this would hardly live up to the word 'generous' in the coalition statement, but we shall just have to wait and see what the emergency Budget brings.

3.7 OTHER POINTS TO CONSIDER

It is worth noting that the coalition statement set out in Section 3.1 does not actually mention Capital Gains Tax. Instead, it refers to 'taxing .... capital gains'.

Am I picking hairs? Maybe not: there are other ways that capital gains could be taxed. Potentially, the Government might fulfil its objective by simply taxing any gains on non-business assets as income – i.e. under Income Tax.

This would be far worse than simply taxing capital gains at Income Tax rates, as it would also mean that these gains would be ineligible for any Capital Gains Tax reliefs, including all the reliefs we looked at in Section 1.5.

We know that Nick Clegg is most keen to tax short-term speculative gains the hardest, so this approach could certainly feature as part of the new regime, such as on assets held for less than a year, for example.

The Annual Exemption

There are rumours that the annual exemption could be radically reduced. I have seen figures as low as £2,500 quoted.

Part of the reason that we have the annual exemption is to reduce the administration involved in dealing with large numbers of small capital gains. With the advance of computer technology, this argument may no longer be valid, so a reduction is a possibility.

Whether it could go as low as £2,500 is yet to be seen but other possibilities might include a small reduction to £10,000 with an ongoing freeze at that level thereafter.

Other Existing Reliefs

Any of the reliefs discussed in Section 1.5 could be amended or even abolished. Certainly, the existing entrepreneurs' relief is likely to be superseded by new reliefs for business assets, as discussed in Section 3.6.

In my view, the other reliefs are more likely to be amended than abolished, but there are no guarantees on anything!

3.8 SUMMARY

Of necessity, this chapter has had to include a great deal of speculation.

We have discussed when the new Capital Gains Tax regime is likely to be introduced, what it will be like, what exemptions will be available and which types of business they are likely to apply to.

Hopefully, you will now have formed your own picture of what the new regime is likely to mean to you. You will probably also have a good idea of whether it is going to be worth taking action to beat the increase which is coming.

For most of the rest of the guide, we will be looking at what action you can take to safeguard your assets from the Capital Gains Tax increase. Before we do, though, we are going to look at some of the factors you will need to consider first.

Chapter 4

Should You Take Action Now?

4.1 LOOK BEFORE YOU LEAP

In this chapter, we will consider some of the drawbacks to taking any sort of action now in order to beat the Capital Gains Tax increase.

The purpose of this is not to talk you out of taking action but to make sure that you are aware of all the factors you will need to take into account.

Always bear in mind that an increase in Capital Gains Tax cannot affect you unless you make any capital gains - and you cannot make any capital gains unless you dispose of an asset.

You therefore always have the simple option of doing nothing: simply hanging on to your assets.

This may not be viable as a permanent solution, as many of your assets may be subject to Inheritance Tax one day, but it could be a reasonable approach in the meantime.

The Capital Gains Tax increase is part of a programme to cut the current deficit: there is every reason to believe that it will not be a permanent feature of the UK tax system and that a return to lower rates of Capital Gains Tax in a few years' time is a strong possibility.

If you take this view, then it may make sense to simply 'wait it out' in some cases.

4.2 KNEE-JERK RESPONSES OR FATAL DELAYS

One of the biggest issues facing us all at the moment is whether to act quickly before the emergency Budget on 22nd June or wait and see what happens in the hope that there will be more time to put together a planned response.

We considered the likelihood of a back-dated or immediate increase in Section 3.2 and we know there are no certainties on this point.

Act quickly and you may beat the increase but you may find that there was actually no need as your own business or investments are not as badly affected as you feared. You may have needlessly created a tax bill for yourself and disrupted a business or a planned investment strategy for no good reason.

Worse still, if the increase is back-dated, you may find that your actions were totally in vain and you have landed yourself with a large tax bill under the new regime (we will look at some possible safeguards against this outcome in Chapter 10).

On the other hand, delaying action until after 22nd June may mean that you are too late to beat the increase if the new regime takes effect immediately.

4.3   TRANSACTION COSTS

It is vital to take the costs of your actions into account.

Selling any type of asset will inevitably give rise to some costs. Whilst these will generally be deductible for Capital Gains Tax purposes, this is really the only practical use that they have if the only reason for making a sale or some other type of disposal is to avoid Capital Gains Tax.

In other words, if your sale or disposal is purely tax driven, the costs arising are just 'dead money' and should be deducted from the tax saving generated in any reckoning of the value of your actions.

Furthermore, if you then go on to re-acquire the same asset, or acquire similar replacement assets, you will also need to factor in the purchase costs involved. (See Section 6.2 regarding the re-acquisition of quoted investments.)

Alternatively, if your spouse or another family member is making the new acquisition, then you will need to factor in their purchase costs.

Either way, those purchase costs may include additional taxes such as Stamp Duty, Stamp Duty Land Tax or VAT. Stamp Duty Land Tax, in particular, is something to be very wary of and we will take a detailed look at some of the issues to be considered in Section 12.1.

As a general point, it is important to remember that many transaction costs are charged on the entire value of the asset, whereas Capital Gains Tax is only payable on your capital gain.

Hence, for example, a 22% Capital Gains Tax saving may initially seem to be beneficial, even in the face of 6% in transaction costs, but if the gain amounts to only £50,000 and the asset is worth £300,000 in total, you would be incurring transactions costs of £18,000 to make a Capital Gains Tax saving of just £11,000 – an overall loss of £7,000!

You may spot that I have ignored any additional Capital Gains Tax saving generated by deducting the transaction costs from sales proceeds, or adding them to any new asset's base cost (as explained in Sections 2.2 and 2.7 respectively). In practice, this should certainly be taken into account, but it will seldom be enough to tip the balance.

4.4   HIDDEN COSTS

In addition to the direct costs of disposal and re-acquisition, you also need to consider the 'hidden costs' associated with the disruption of a business or a planned investment strategy.

In the next couple of sections we are going to look at some issues specific to particular businesses or investments but, on top of these, there is always the effective cost of your own time (which can never be recovered). There will often also be additional accountancy fees in dealing with your next accounts or tax return due to the added complexity caused by your transactions.

Another hidden cost which might apply to most types of asset is the reduction in value caused by trying to make a quick sale. This is particularly relevant to anyone trying to push sales through before the emergency Budget on 22nd June. Stock market values may also be depressed if large numbers of investors are selling off investments just before then.

If the Capital Gains Tax increase is deferred until 6th April 2011, this 'quick sale' effect will be less pronounced to begin with, but may resume even greater proportions as we draw near to the fateful day!

4.5 STOCK MARKET INVESTMENTS

For stock market investments, the direct costs involved in a sale and re-acquisition are not generally too significant (but see Section 6.2 regarding the tax effect of re-acquiring the same investment after less than 31 days).

Broker's fees generally only amount to £10 to £15 per transaction and the Stamp Duty on new purchases is just 0.5%.

The greatest 'hidden cost' however, could be the bid offer spread (i.e. the difference between the buying and selling price).

For large companies with a full quotation, this may be negligible, but for smaller, thinly traded companies, especially AIM companies, the spread can be 5% to 10% or more.

In effect, by selling one set of shares and acquiring a new set, whether in the same company or not, you will be suffering the cost of the bid offer spread a second time. For those smaller companies with the greater spread, this could easily eat up any Capital Gains Tax savings. Remember that you will suffer the spread on the entire value of your investment, not just on the capital gain.

There may also be a significant element of 'investment risk'. As explained in Section 6.2, you may need to wait at least 31 days before you can re-acquire the same investment and you could easily find that you have lost out on a significant amount of capital growth during that period. Conversely, of course, you might benefit from a fall in value during that same period, but you'll have to weigh up your chances for yourself on this.

4.6 PROPERTY

Property probably suffers from the highest transaction costs of any type of asset and is also subject to a great deal of 'hidden costs'.

When selling a property, you will generally incur legal fees, estate agents' fees and advertising costs.

Purchasing a property will lead to more legal fees, as well as survey fees and, of course, Stamp Duty Land Tax (see Section 12.1 for details).

Where the old property, the new one, or both, are partly financed by way of mortgages, there will be further costs to consider: early redemption penalties on the old mortgage and mortgage arrangement fees on the new one (as well as further legal fees and survey fees).

Furthermore, you may be unable to obtain a new mortgage at as good a rate as your existing mortgage, leaving you with higher interest costs in future. You may also have to borrow more in order to fund all of your transactions costs and the Capital Gains Tax bill on the sale of your old property. Worst of all, you may not even be able to get a new mortgage in the current climate!

Amongst the hidden costs, the issue of losing value by trying to make a quick sale is particularly relevant to property. You may have to sell at a significant discount, perhaps at an auction, or to a property investor looking for a 'BMV' (below market value) purchase.

Residential properties with sitting tenants can also be particularly difficult to sell.

Furthermore, from a commercial perspective, you could lose a good long-term tenant by selling an existing property and then face the risk of voids and poorer quality short-term tenants in any new property, thus reducing your rental income significantly.

4.7 TRANSFERS VERSUS OPEN MARKET SALES

Many of the costs discussed over the last few sections can be avoided, or at least reduced, by transferring an asset to a family member, a company or a trust, using some of the planning techniques discussed in later chapters, rather than making an open market sale of the asset.

This is particularly true where you are also seeking to either re-acquire the same asset or purchase a similar replacement asset. By transferring the existing asset within the family or to a company or trust under your control, you can avoid the need to do this.

However, transfers do have two distinct disadvantages which you need to be aware of.

Firstly, as explained in Section 2.3, transfers to your spouse will seldom be effective for Capital Gains Tax planning purposes.

Secondly, a transfer by way of gift or in exchange for consideration left outstanding as a loan will often create a Capital Gains Tax liability, but will not generate any cash proceeds from which to pay it. Hence, you will have to fund the Capital Gains Tax cost arising out of other resources, possibly forcing you to make some open market sales alongside your transfers.

4.8   LOSS OF CONTROL

A transfer of an asset to another family member will result in you personally losing control over that asset. This is particularly relevant to business assets, such as business premises or private company shares.

This particular problem can often be avoided by transferring assets to a trust or into your own private company. We will look at these solutions in detail in Chapters 8 and 9 respectively.

4.9   LOSS OF INCOME

Another problem with transferring assets to another individual is the fact that you will lose the income derived from those assets.

You cannot circumvent this by simply arranging for the future income to be paid back to you. This would create what is known as a 'settlement' and could also potentially undo all of your tax planning.

In practice, the best ways to transfer assets under the current low Capital Gains Tax regime without losing the future income from the assets concerned are again to use a trust or a company.

4.10   REDUCTION IN CAPITAL

Whether you make an open market sale or an asset transfer, you will generally be creating a Capital Gains Tax liability.

Although this is the purpose of the exercise and, if all goes well, should be at the current low rate of 18%, your tax bill will inevitably eat into your available capital, leaving you less money for new investments and thus generating less income in the future as a result.

For example, let us suppose you have an investment portfolio which is worth £200,000 and stands at a capital gain of £100,000.

If you've already used your annual exemption elsewhere, then a sale of your portfolio would give rise to a Capital Gains Tax bill of £18,000, even under the current regime.

This leaves you with only £182,000 to reinvest or, say, around £181,500 after transaction costs. You will then have to pay 0.5% in Stamp Duty on any new investments, possibly amounting to around £900. Taking the bid offer spread (see Section 4.5) and a few more transaction charges on your purchases into account, your new investment portfolio will be worth around £180,000.

In other words, your tax planning will have wiped 10% off the value of your investments – decimated them, in fact!

All other things being equal, this, in turn, will probably also reduce your future income by 10%.

This might suggest that you could be better off simply sitting tight and hanging on to your assets until we return to a lower Capital Gains Tax regime again one day.

But how long can you sit tight? If the high Capital Gains Tax regime lasts for a long time, you may end up wishing that you'd paid that 18% tax after all. (For a worked example that illustrates this point, see Section 6.3.)

Alternatively, you may have been planning to sell your assets in the near future anyway?

4.11 WHAT IF YOU ARE PLANNING TO SELL UP ANYWAY?

Many of the issues discussed in this chapter are only relevant to someone contemplating a sale or transfer of an asset purely as a tax planning measure to avoid the Capital Gains Tax increase.

If, on the other hand, you are planning to sell an asset anyway, regardless of the Capital Gains Tax increase, then the only real issues for you revolve around timing: are you better off selling under the current regime or the new regime?

The issues discussed in Section 4.2 will lie at the heart of your decision making: make a quick sale before 22nd June, or wait and see what the emergency Budget brings?

Transaction costs will not generally be an issue, as you are going to incur these anyway. Unless, that is, you expect them to change significantly depending on the timing of your sale.

Most hidden costs will also generally be irrelevant, although the possible loss of value caused by trying to force through a quick sale may remain an issue, especially if you decide to push a sale through before 22nd June.

Here though, there is a way that you may be able to 'have your cake and eat it'. By following some of the techniques set out in Chapters 7 to 9, you can create a capital gain under the current regime without having to force through a quick sale on the open market.

Later, when conditions are right for you to realise the asset's full value on the open market, you can sell the asset and only suffer the new increased Capital Gains Tax rate on the extra increase in value arising after the earlier transfer.

In Chapters 7 to 9, we will see some examples which demonstrate just how much this could save you under the right circumstances.

Chapter 5

Creating a Capital Gain

5.1 WHY DO WE WANT TO CREATE A CAPITAL GAIN?

By creating a capital gain now, we can shelter some or all of an asset's capital growth to date from the new Capital Gains Tax regime (assuming, of course, that the new regime is not back-dated).

In most cases, this will involve actually paying some Capital Gains Tax now. We have discussed some of the potential drawbacks to this in Section 4.10 but, in the chapters which follow, we will see just how significant the potential long-term savings may be.

In other cases, it may be possible to create a capital gain now, but avoid or reduce the Capital Gains Tax payable at this stage, whilst still achieving long-term savings. We will look at some of these opportunities in detail later.

5.2 THE FOUR MAIN WAYS TO CREATE A CAPITAL GAIN

Over the next four chapters, we are going to explore the four main methods for creating a capital gain. These are:

- Open market sales
- A transfer to another individual (e.g. your adult child)
- A transfer to a trust
- A transfer to a company

Each method has different advantages, disadvantages and other implications and the best method for you will depend on your own circumstances and your plans for the future. We will examine all of these issues over the next four chapters.

What all of the methods have in common, however, is the ability to shelter capital growth to date from any future Capital Gains Tax increases by creating a capital gain under the current regime – provided, as always, that the increases are not back-dated.

5.3 TRANSFERS TO SPOUSES

As explained in Section 2.3, a direct transfer of an asset to your spouse is deemed to take place on a 'no gain/no loss' basis for Capital Gains Tax purposes and will not generally create a capital gain.

There are, however, other ways to effectively transfer assets to your spouse and still achieve the desired result.

One method is to simply sell assets on the open market which your spouse then re-purchases, again on the open market.

For sales of quoted shares and securities, this has the advantage that your spouse can make the re-purchase immediately and does not have to wait for the required 31 days (see Section 6.2).

Another possible method is to use a trust. We will explore this option in Chapter 8.

Non-Resident Spouses

The 'no gain/no loss' rule continues to apply where your spouse is non-UK resident and non-UK ordinarily resident and thus generally exempt from UK Capital Gains Tax (see Section 1.3).

A transfer to such a spouse could therefore be a very effective way to avoid UK Capital Gains Tax.

It will, however, require a fairly unusual set of circumstances, as you would generally need to be living in different countries for a significant proportion of the time and yet not be regarded as 'separated'.

There are also two important issues to be wary of.

Firstly, as your spouse is resident in another country, they may be subject to foreign tax on capital gains (as explained in the 'Scope of this Guide').

Secondly, if your spouse is not already non-UK resident and non-UK ordinarily resident at the time that the asset is transferred, this method will generally be ineffective.

Emigrating Spouses

Where an asset has been transferred between spouses and the transferee spouse subsequently becomes neither UK resident nor UK ordinarily resident, the transferred asset is treated for UK Capital Gains Tax purposes as if it still belonged to the transferor spouse.

In other words, a transfer to a spouse who is currently subject to UK Capital Gains Tax, but who then subsequently emigrates, is completely ineffective in avoiding Capital Gains Tax. (Unless, of course, the transferor also emigrates themselves – see Section 11.2.)

Chapter 6

Open Market Sales

6.1 KEEPING IT SIMPLE

Our first method for creating a capital gain is to simply sell assets on the open market.

This is well suited to quoted investments, which can usually be sold quickly and easily.

Properties and businesses generally take somewhat longer to sell, especially if you want to get a fair price.

For properties, the issues covered in Section 4.6 need to be considered. Landlords, in particular, need to consider these issues carefully, as a sale of property is effectively also a major change to your business and has far-reaching implications.

Selling a business can take longest of all and should rarely be undertaken purely to create a capital gain. Unless you are intent on selling the business in any case, the other methods covered in the next three chapters will generally be far more appropriate.

6.2 REPURCHASES AND REPLACEMENTS

The difficulty with an open market sale is that you have lost your original asset. For businesses or properties, it will generally be totally impractical to repurchase the same asset, so this method is only suitable when you are happy to either go without the asset in future or to invest in a suitable replacement.

Open market sales of businesses and properties are therefore generally only worth contemplating for those wishing to sell their assets in any case.

When you sell quoted investments, you can either repurchase the same investments or buy replacements. In either case, you will need to make allowances for your Capital Gains Tax bill, although it may be some time before this is payable.

You will need to be careful when repurchasing the same quoted shares or securities. As explained in Section 2.9, re-acquiring the same shares within 30 days will alter the way in which your capital gain is calculated. This could actually wipe out your capital gain, thus defeating the object of the exercise!

Example

Jack owns 1,000 shares in Senkrah plc which he purchased in 1983 for £1 each. They are now worth £101 each, so he decides to sell them so that he can pay Capital Gains Tax at just 18% on his capital growth to date of £100,000.

Foolishly, however, Jack re-purchases 1,000 shares in Senkrah plc just 28 days later at a price of £100 per share.

For Capital Gains Tax purposes, he is treated as if the shares he sold were the shares he re-acquired 28 days later, giving him a capital gain of just £1,000 instead of the gain of £100,000 he had planned to create.

The biggest problem, however, is that the shares he now holds are treated as if they were his original shares and his base cost for these shares is therefore just £1 per share.

Waiting 31 days before making your re-acquisition will ensure you create your capital gain as planned and, more importantly, will also ensure that the base cost for your new shares is their actual purchase price. The drawback, however, is that this exposes you to the investment risk which we talked about in Section 4.5.

A good way to get around this problem is for your spouse or partner to make the repurchase instead of you. In this way, as a couple, you will have kept hold of your investment but also created the uplift in base cost which you need.

For small investments, you could also make the repurchase via an ISA (except for AIM shares, which cannot be purchased through an ISA unless they also have a dual listing on a recognised stock exchange overseas).

Other methods include making the repurchase through a trust or a company, although in many cases it may be better to simply transfer the investments directly.

6.3 POTENTIAL SAVINGS

To demonstrate the potential savings of making open market sales before the Capital Gains Tax increase takes effect, let's look at a detailed example.

In this example, I will assume that the Capital Gains Tax regime remains unchanged for the remainder of the current tax year but that, from 6th April 2011, gains on non-business assets are taxed at Income Tax rates (but not the 50% 'super tax' rate), and the annual exemption is reduced to just £5,000.

Example

Donna and Annod both pay higher rate Income Tax at 40% and each own a stock market portfolio worth £250,000 with original base costs totalling £50,000 in each case.

In March 2011, Donna sells her portfolio, realising total capital gains of £200,000. After deducting her annual exemption of £10,100, she suffers Capital Gains Tax at 18% on the remaining £189,900. Her tax bill thus amounts to £34,182.

Putting the money for her tax bill to one side, Donna is left with £215,818 to reinvest. £1,075 of this is used to pay Stamp Duty at 0.5% on her new investments, so her new portfolio is actually worth £214,743.

Over the next couple of years, Donna and Annod's portfolios both grow in value by 10%. At this point, each of them sells off their entire portfolio. Their Capital Gains Tax bills are calculated as follows:

	Donna £	Annod £
Total sale proceeds	236,218	275,000
Less base cost	215,818	50,000
	20,400	225,000
Annual exemption	5,000	5,000
Taxable gains	15,400	220,000

Even at 40%, Donna's Capital Gains Tax bill will amount to a mere £6,160. Annod, on the other hand, will face a bill of £88,000.

More importantly, though, Donna will be left with net after-tax proceeds of £230,058 (£236,218 - £6,160), whereas Annod's will amount to just £187,000 (£275,000 - £88,000).

In this example, the investor who took action now and sold off their portfolio under the current Capital Gains Tax regime has ended up more than £43,000, or over 23%, better off.

This, of course, is based on a situation where the investors sell their portfolios in the near future, after further capital growth of just 10%.

In the longer term, the loss of value caused by creating a Capital Gains Tax bill in 2010/11 will begin to have a bigger impact. As discussed in Section 4.10, this loss of value will also generally lead to reduced income in future years.

Nevertheless, focussing on capital values alone, it would actually take further capital growth of more than 200% before Annod eventually ended up with more net sales proceeds than Donna.

In fact, in this particular example, and assuming a compound growth rate of 5%, it would actually take 24 years!

6.4   YOU MAY HAVE LONGER THAN YOU THINK

As we know, it can take a little time to sell a property or a business at a fair price so there is a serious issue in getting these sales completed in time to beat the Capital Gains Tax increase.

It is worth remembering, however, that the date of disposal for Capital Gains Tax purposes is the date of an unconditional sales contract and not the date of entry, date of completion, etc.

Hence, it is only necessary to have the sales contract in place before the Capital Gains Tax increase. In some cases, this could give you just enough extra time to make your sale under the current Capital Gains Tax regime after all.

Chapter 7

Transfers to Another Individual

7.1 KEEPING IT IN THE FAMILY

The simplest method for creating a capital gain without selling an asset on the open market is to transfer the asset to another individual.

As explained in Section 2.4, a transfer to a 'connected person' other than your spouse will be deemed to take place at open market value. In Section 2.6, we also saw that transfers to other people will often produce the same result.

Transfers of this type are suitable for most types of asset, provided that you are not concerned with the loss of control or the loss of income, as discussed in Sections 4.8 and 4.9 respectively.

A loss of control is a particular issue for business assets: you may not want your children or other people to have control over your business. On the other hand, in some cases, it may be the right time to pass over control to the next generation, so if this can be combined with some Capital Gains Tax planning, then all well and good.

Minority shareholdings in private companies can often be transferred without an overall loss of control over the company itself and this is often a good first step towards eventually passing over control to the next generation.

Many business assets can be passed on free from Capital Gains Tax by claiming holdover relief (see Section 7.5). However, this leaves the historic growth in the asset's value fully exposed to Capital Gains Tax and thus defeats the object if you are actually trying to avoid Capital Gains Tax on a sale in the foreseeable future.

In other situations, of course, holdover relief is invaluable and if you see the assets remaining 'in the family' for a long time to come, it may make more sense to claim it.

Holdover relief can also be used as a means to 'hedge your bets' or to come up with a compromise solution if you can't afford to trigger the entire capital gain on an asset at the moment. We will look at these uses for the relief later on in Sections 7.6, 7.7 and 10.2.

The loss of income could be a problem when assets are transferred to any person other than your partner. In the case of rental income, however, there is a potential solution, which we will look at in Section 7.8.

If there are still issues regarding the loss of control or loss of income, which cannot be resolved under any of the methods discussed here, then you will need to consider using a trust or a company.

7.2　WHO CAN YOU TRANSFER ASSETS TO?

You can generally create a capital gain by transferring assets to any other adult individual apart from your spouse.

As long as either they are a connected person (see Appendix C), or the transfer is not made 'at arm's length', the deemed sales proceeds will be the current market value of the asset and, more importantly, this will also become the transferee's base cost.

You must pass over genuine beneficial title to the asset, however, so the transferee does need to be someone who you genuinely want to have the asset.

Beyond that, the choice is yours, but some of the more popular choices include your:

- Unmarried partner
- Fiancé/fiancée or intended future civil partner
- Adult children
- Siblings
- Parents
- Friend

A transfer to your fiancé/fiancée or future civil partner must take place before the date of your marriage or registration of your civil partnership in order to create the capital gain as intended.

As explained in Section 2.4, a transfer to a separated spouse after the end of the tax year in which separation occurs would also create a capital gain. This will not always be appropriate but, in some instances, it could be seen as a means to protect the value of family assets for the benefit of minor children.

Transfers to parents are effective for creating a capital gain but this does mean that the asset has been passed to the older generation which may be a bad idea for Inheritance Tax purposes (the value of the parent's estate is increased, thus potentially leading to a larger Inheritance Tax bill on their death).

In theory, transfers to minor children could be used to create capital gains but there are numerous legal and other difficulties, so it will generally be better to use a trust.

7.3   POTENTIAL SAVINGS

The potential savings which might be achieved by transferring an asset to another individual in order to create a capital gain under the current regime can be illustrated by way of an example.

In this example, I will assume that the Capital Gains Tax regime remains unchanged for the remainder of the current tax year but that, from 6th April 2011, capital gains are taxed at Income Tax rates (but not the 50% 'super tax' rate), the annual exemption is reduced to £5,000 and no exemptions are available for rental properties.

Example

Colin has an investment property which he bought some years ago for £100,000 and which is now worth £280,000. He would like to be able to benefit from the current 18% rate of Capital Gains Tax on his existing gain but he also wants to keep the property in the family for a few more years.

Colin therefore transfers the property to his adult daughter Bonnie. This is treated as a sale of the property for its market value of £280,000, giving Colin a capital gain of £180,000. After deducting his annual exemption of £10,100, he is subject to Capital Gains Tax at 18% on £169,900, giving him a tax bill of £30,582.

A few years later, Bonnie sells the property for £350,000. From this, she can deduct her base cost of £280,000: i.e. the market value of the property when Colin gave it to her. This leaves her with a capital gain of £70,000, from which she can deduct her annual exemption of £5,000, leaving her with a taxable gain of £65,000.

If Bonnie is already a higher rate taxpayer, she will pay Capital Gains Tax at 40% on this gain, i.e. £26,000. Between them, Colin and Bonnie have therefore paid a total of £56,582 in Capital Gains Tax.

If, however, Colin had retained the property himself until the time of sale, he would have had a capital gain of £250,000. Deducting his annual exemption of £5,000 would leave him with a taxable gain of £245,000. As a higher rate taxpayer, his Capital Gains Tax bill, at 40%, would therefore be £98,000.

By making a transfer under the current low Capital Gains Tax regime, this family has saved £41,418 (£98,000 - £56,582), which represents almost 12% of their property's value: a sizeable saving.

Most of the saving comes by avoiding the increase in Capital Gains Tax rates on the property's historical growth in value. The existing gain of £180,000 has been taxed at 18% instead of 40%, thus saving the family £39,600 (£180,000 x 22%). On top of this, a small additional saving is produced because Colin uses his 2010/11 annual exemption (£10,100 x 18% = £1,818).

The major drawback, of course, is the fact that Colin faces a tax bill of £30,582 in January 2012 without any sale proceeds to pay it from. In other words, the long-term saving is achieved at a severe cashflow disadvantage!

7.4 GREATER SAVINGS

The example in the previous section is based on the assumption that the 50% 'super tax' rate will not apply to capital gains. Let's hope this is correct but, if not, the savings could be even greater.

The savings may also be greater if an asset is transferred to a basic rate taxpayer with little or no income of their own.

If capital gains are indeed to be taxed at Income Tax rates, a basic rate taxpayer would only pay Capital Gains Tax at 20% on at least some of their capital gains.

Example Revisited

In the tax year that she sells the property, Bonnie's taxable income is fully covered by her personal allowance.

The basic rate band is £35,000 (say), so Bonnie's Capital Gains Tax bill on her taxable gain of £65,000 (see Section 7.3) is made up as follows:

£35,000 @ 20% =   £7,000
£30,000 @ 40% =   £12,000

Total: £19,000

This means that the family has now only paid a total of £49,582 (£30,582 + £19,000) instead of the £98,000 that Colin would have paid if he had retained the property, saving £48,418 and almost halving their tax bill!

As we can see, there may be even greater tax saving opportunities available if assets are transferred to basic rate taxpayers.

7.5 BUSINESS ASSETS AND HOLDOVER RELIEF

As explained in Section 1.5, it is possible to hold over the gain arising on a gift, or sale at below market value, of qualifying business assets.

For these purposes, 'qualifying business assets' include:

- Assets used in the owner's own trading business
- Furnished holiday letting properties (provided that the furnished holiday letting regime is still in force: see Section 3.4)
- Shares in an unquoted trading company ('unquoted' does not include shares traded on AIM)
- A holding of at least 5% of a quoted trading company.

To be a trading company, the underlying business must not include any 'substantial' element of non-trading activities. This is usually taken to mean that non-trading activities amount to no more than 20% of the business.

Note that, once made, a holdover relief claim is irrevocable.

As discussed in Section 7.1, where holdover relief is available on a transfer of assets and these assets are likely to be retained by the transferee for many years to come, then it will generally make sense to claim the relief rather than trigger a Capital Gains Tax liability now.

It is also worth bearing in mind that some assets which are currently eligible for holdover relief may also be eligible for new exemptions for 'entrepreneurial business activities', as discussed in Chapter 3, meaning that they will not be exposed to any Capital Gains Tax increase in any case.

On the other hand, however, as discussed in Section 3.4, there is the possibility that future exemptions will not be available to every asset which is currently eligible for holdover relief. If so, you may wish to consider making a transfer without claiming the relief, in order to avoid the Capital Gains Tax increase. It may actually possible to 'hedge your bets' a bit here and we will look at this in more detail in Section 10.2.

If you make a straightforward gift of an asset without claiming holdover relief then, unless entrepreneurs' relief is available, your position will be much the same as the example in Section 7.3, subject to any possible exemptions which might apply on the ultimate sale. (We will look at the impact of entrepreneurs' relief on asset transfers in Section 7.7.)

If you do claim holdover relief, the transferee will not benefit from any increase in base cost and the asset's historical growth in value will be fully exposed to the new Capital Gains Tax regime. This might still produce a small saving where the transferee is a basic rate taxpayer, however.

Example Part 3

Let us now assume that Colin's property which cost £100,000 and is now worth £280,000 is actually his business premises. He gifts the property to Bonnie and they jointly elect to hold over the gain arising of £180,000.

Later, Bonnie sells the property for £350,000. Because of the holdover relief claim, she can only deduct a base cost of £100,000, leaving her with a capital gain of £250,000. Deducting her annual exemption of £5,000 (say), she is left with a taxable gain of £245,000.

As in Section 7.4, we will assume that gains are taxed at Income Tax rates, Bonnie's income is fully covered by her personal allowance, and the basic rate band is £35,000. Bonnie's Capital Gains Tax bill is therefore as follows:

£35,000 @ 20% =   £7,000
£210,000 @ 40% =   £84,000

Total: £91,000

If Colin, as a higher rate taxpayer, had sold the property, his Capital Gains Tax bill would have been £98,000 (see Section 7.3). A small saving of £7,000 has therefore still been achieved without the cashflow disadvantage of a Capital Gains Tax bill in January 2012.

We are assuming here that there would not be any exemptions available on the ultimate sale of the property. As discussed above, however, the fact that it qualifies for holdover relief means that there could be. This could render the whole exercise pretty pointless.

Worse still, if Colin would have been entitled to an exemption if he had retained the property but Bonnie is not, the transfer may have completely backfired and created a significantly greater Capital Gains Tax bill!

Such a transfer should therefore probably only be contemplated if it seems highly probable that the asset will lose its status as a qualifying business asset in future or will not qualify for any exemptions under the new Capital Gains Tax regime.

7.6 PARTIAL HOLDOVER RELIEF

It is possible to obtain a form of partial holdover relief by selling qualifying business assets for less than their market value rather than gifting them outright.

Because this is not a transfer 'at arm's length', the deemed sales proceeds are still the asset's open market value, but the transferor and transferee can jointly elect to hold over the part of the capital gain in excess of the actual sales proceeds.

Naturally, all of the concerns set out in Section 7.5 above should still be taken into account, but this does provide the opportunity to limit the tax charge arising on the original transfer to fit your budget.

Note that, as there will now be some actual consideration for the transfer, this could give rise to Stamp Duty Land Tax in the case of properties (see Section 12.1 for details), or to Stamp Duty at 0.5% in the case of shares.

The sale consideration does not need to be payable immediately and could, in fact, be left outstanding as a loan. It is sensible to ensure that both the sale consideration and any loan are formally documented.

Example

Barbara owns the entire issued share capital of Diggers Limited, a property development company. She is concerned that her shares might not qualify for any exemptions under the new Capital Gains Tax regime, so she wants to transfer a 49% shareholding in the company to her daughter Susan.

Barbara's base cost for 49% of her shares is just £49 and they are worth £1,000,000. She has already used up both her annual exemption and her £2m limit for entrepreneurs' relief (see Section 1.5) so, without claiming any holdover relief, a straight gift of the shares to Susan would give rise to a Capital Gains Tax bill of £179,991.

Barbara can only afford a maximum Capital Gains Tax bill of £100,000 without causing critical disruption to her business so, instead of an outright gift, she sells a 49% shareholding to Susan for £555,605.

Barbara and Susan then jointly elect to hold over the additional gain of £444,395 in excess of the actual sale price.

Barbara's Capital Gains Tax calculation is then as follows:

	£
Deemed sales proceeds (market value)	1,000,000
Less base cost	49
	999,951
Less held over gain	444,395
Taxable gain	555,556
Capital Gains Tax at 18% thereon:	£100,000

Susan will have to pay Stamp Duty of £2,780 (0.5% of £555,605), giving her a base cost for the shares of £558,385: i.e. their market value of £1,000,000 plus the Stamp Duty less the held over gain of £444,395.

As we can see, by fixing the sale price below market value and claiming partial holdover relief for the difference, the transferor has been able to choose how much Capital Gains Tax to pay on the transfer.

This has also effectively fixed the transferee's base cost which ends up being the actual sale price plus any incidental purchase costs (in this case, Stamp Duty of £2,780).

Example Continued

Several years later, Barbara and Susan sell the company for a total of £3m. Sadly, it turns out that Barbara was right and shares in Digger Limited are not eligible for any exemptions under the new regime [note: this is just an assumption!].

Susan receives proceeds of £1,470,000 for her 49% shareholding from which she can deduct her base cost of £558,385 and her annual exemption of £5,000 (say), leaving her with a taxable gain of £906,615 and a Capital Gains Tax bill, at 40%, of £362,646.

Barbara will, of course, have a Capital Gains Tax bill on her remaining 51% shareholding, but this is the same as it always would have been without the transfer. What Barbara has avoided is a further capital gain of £1,469,951 (£1,470,000 - £49) on the shares she previously transferred to Susan. This would have increased her Capital Gains Tax bill by a further £587,980 (at 40%).

The overall net tax saved by the family is therefore as follows:

	£
Tax avoided by Barbara on final sale	587,980
Less:	
Tax paid by Barbara on transfer	100,000
Stamp Duty paid by Susan	2,780
Tax paid by Susan on final sale	362,646
Overall net saving:	122,554

This is less than the theoretical maximum saving which could have been achieved if Barbara had simply gifted the shares to Susan (£221,989); but what use would that have been if Barbara and Digger Limited had been ruined by a bigger Capital Gains Tax bill in January 2012 than Barbara could afford?

Minor Savings

Where an asset is eligible for holdover relief and the owner has not used their annual exemption elsewhere, it will be possible to produce some minor savings without giving rise to any immediate Capital Gains Tax liability.

This is done by simply selling the asset for £10,100 more than your original base cost.

You then claim partial holdover relief which reduces your gain to £10,100 and this is covered by your annual exemption.

This then provides the new owner with a £10,100 increase in base cost which may yield a saving of up to £4,040 under the new regime.

Where you are also eligible for entrepreneurs' relief (see Section 7.7), you could sell the asset for £18,180 more than your original base cost and still avoid any immediate Capital Gains Tax liability by claiming partial holdover relief.

The new owner now has a £18,180 increase in base cost which could save up to £7,272 under the new regime **if** the asset is not eligible for any form of exemption.

7.7 ENTREPRENEUR'S RELIEF

Assets currently eligible for entrepreneurs' relief may be subject to an effective Capital Gains Tax rate of just 10%. The basic mechanics of how the relief works were set out in Section 1.5.

The relief is only available under fairly limited circumstances, generally involving the disposal or cessation of a business, or an interest in a business. Broadly speaking, entrepreneurs' relief is available on the disposal of:

i) The whole or part of a qualifying business
ii) Assets formerly used in a qualifying business which has ceased or been disposed of
iii) Shares or securities in a 'personal company'

A qualifying business for this purpose is generally a trade, although, once again, qualifying furnished holiday letting businesses may also qualify if the furnished holiday letting regime is still in force (see Section 3.4).

A 'part' of a business can only be counted for these purposes if it is capable of operating as a going concern in its own right, but an 'interest' in a business, such as a partnership share, may qualify.

A disposal of assets formerly used in a qualifying business must take place within three years after the cessation or disposal of the business.

In all cases, the individual making the disposal must have owned the qualifying business for at least a year prior to its disposal, or cessation, as the case may be.

The definition of a 'personal company' for the purposes of entrepreneurs' relief is broadly as follows:

  i)   The individual holds at least 5% of the ordinary share capital
  ii) The holding under (i) provides at least 5% of the voting rights
  iii) The company is a trading company (using the same 20% rule as we saw in Section 7.5)
  iv) The individual is an officer or employee of the company (an 'officer' includes a non-executive director or company secretary)

Each of these rules must be satisfied for the period of at least one year prior to the disposal in question or, where the company has ceased trading, for at least one year prior to the cessation. In the latter case, the disposal must again take place within three years after cessation.

Entrepreneurs' relief may sometimes also extend to assets owned personally but used in the trade of a 'personal company', or a partnership in which the owner is a partner. A number of restrictions apply, however. Broadly, the relief is only available where the owner is also disposing of their shares in the company, or interest in the partnership, and is also restricted where any payment has been received for the use of the assets concerned after 5th April 2008.

Planning Implications

As discussed in Section 3.6, it is probable that entrepreneurs' relief in its current form will no longer apply under the new Capital Gains Tax regime.

However, it is also quite possible that many of the disposals which would currently qualify for entrepreneurs' relief will also qualify for some of those 'generous exemptions' we talked about in Chapter 3.

This creates a dilemma for anyone with assets currently eligible for entrepreneurs' relief. Should they 'cash in' the current effective rate of 10% while they still can, or should they 'sit tight' in the hope that equally, or even more generous exemptions will be available in future?

At present, I cannot answer this dilemma for you but, if you do decide that it would make sense to realise capital gains at the current effective rate of 10%, without paying any Capital Gains Tax at the full rate of 18%, a partial holdover relief claim may provide the means to do it.

In the example which follows, I am assuming that the Capital Gains Tax regime remains unchanged for the remainder of the current tax year, including the £2m lifetime limit for entrepreneurs' relief. I am also assuming that, from 6th April 2011, gains will be taxed at Income Tax rates (but not the 50% 'super tax' rate), and widget trading businesses will not be eligible for any exemptions. I am also ignoring the annual exemption for the sake of illustration.

Example

Leila runs a successful widget trading business through her company, Jameson Limited. Her shares in the company qualify for entrepreneurs' relief and originally cost just £1,000.

Although the company is worth £7m, Leila sells her shares to her son Navin for £2,001,000. For Capital Gains Tax purposes, Leila has a gain, based on the market value of her shares, of almost £7m, but she and Navin can jointly elect to hold over the part of the gain in excess of the actual sale price. This leaves Leila with a taxable gain of just £2m which, because she is entitled to entrepreneurs' relief, will be taxed at an effective rate of just 10%.

As we can see, the partial holdover relief claim has enabled Leila to benefit from the current beneficial 10% rate on the first £2m of gains qualifying for entrepreneurs' relief without having to pay any further tax at this stage.

Navin will pay Stamp Duty (at 0.5%) of £10,005, giving him a base cost of £2,011,005 (£2,001,000 + £10,005).

Example Continued

A few years later, Navin sells Jameson Limited for £8m. This gives him a capital gain of £5,988,995 and a Capital Gains Tax bill, at 40%, of £2,395,598. Added to the £200,000 (£2m x 10%) in Capital Gains Tax which Leila paid on the transfer and the £10,005 in Stamp Duty paid by Navin, this produces a total cost of £2,605,603.

If Leila had still owned the company at this stage, her Capital Gains Tax bill would have been £3,199,600. The transfer has therefore given the family an overall net saving of £593,997.

Under these circumstances, an outright gift of shares to Navin, or a sale at undervalue with no holdover relief claim, would have produced a greater saving because Leila would then have sheltered the entire current value of £7m from the new Capital Gains Tax regime. This would have come at a high cost: a further £899,820 in Capital Gains Tax due in January 2012; but would have yielded an overall net saving of £1,699,780 in the long run.

On the other hand, however, if widget trading businesses are eligible for some form of exemption under the new regime, then creating additional capital gains taxed at 18% under the current regime could prove disastrous.

Clearly, this is the point of using a sale at below market value and a partial holdover relief claim: it enables you to 'cash in' the part of the gain currently taxed at an effective rate of 10% without paying any Capital Gains Tax at the full rate of 18%.

If, in the end, your business is eligible for some form of exemption which produces an effective Capital Gains Tax rate somewhere between 10% and 18%, this will turn out to have been the best solution.

7.8   JOINTLY HELD PROPERTY

Where two people own rental property jointly, and they are neither a married couple nor a registered civil partnership, they can agree to share the rental income in a different proportion to their beneficial title in the property.

This means that you could transfer a joint share in a rental property to another individual but then agree that you retain a large proportion, or even all, of the rental income.

Furthermore, property held as tenants in common (or 'pro indivisio' in Scotland) can be held in any proportion you wish, not just 50/50; so you could transfer most of the capital value of the property in order to create a capital gain, shelter most of the current value from the Capital Gains Tax increase, and yet still retain most of the income.

Your initial rental profit sharing agreement should be made as soon as possible after the transfer, but must not be a condition of that transfer. Thereafter, any changes should be agreed before the beginning of the relevant tax year. It is wise to use a written document to evidence the agreement and it is also important to have a rationale for the agreed split. For example, one joint owner might agree to allow the other joint owner to take 80% of the income on the basis that they are responsible for the management of the properties.

For Income Tax purposes, you will be taxed on your agreed profit share.

It is essential that the transferee agrees to the profit sharing agreement of their own free will and is also free to demand a return to their full beneficial entitlement in the future.

7.9 INHERITANCE TAX

Gifts or sales of assets at below market value to another individual represent a 'transfer of value' for Inheritance Tax purposes.

They are, however, also a 'potentially exempt transfer'. This means that, provided you survive at least seven years after making the transfer, the asset will be safely excluded from your estate for Inheritance Tax purposes.

If you should die within that period, however, the value of the asset at the date of transfer will effectively be counted within your estate for Inheritance Tax purposes (although any actual consideration charged on the transfer can be deducted).

None of this alters the Capital Gains Tax consequences of the original transfer and, although some Inheritance Tax may be due, it will be no more than would have arisen in any case. An early death may, however, mean that your family will be missing out on the 'uplift on death' discussed in Section 2.12.

In other words, if you would still have held the asset at the time of your death had it not been for the transfer, then that transfer may have created an unnecessary additional Capital Gains Tax bill.

For more details see the Taxcafe.co.uk guide *'How to Avoid Inheritance Tax'*.

7.10 TRANSFERS TO NON-RESIDENT INDIVIDUALS

Holdover relief cannot be claimed on a transfer to an individual who is neither UK resident nor UK ordinarily resident.

In other words, it is not usually possible to get an asset out of the UK Capital Gains Tax 'net' completely tax free by transferring it to a non-resident (but see Section 5.3 regarding transfers to non-resident spouses).

Nevertheless, whilst such a transfer will come at a cost, it is still a very effective way to shelter historic growth in value from the Capital Gains Tax increase and, at the same time, shelter future growth in value from UK Capital Gains Tax altogether!

Example

Let us assume that the facts are exactly the same as the example in Section 7.3, except that Bonnie is non-UK resident and non-UK ordinarily resident.

As before, Colin will incur a Capital Gains Tax liability of £30,582 on the original transfer to Bonnie.

However, when Bonnie later sells the property, she will have no UK Capital Gains Tax to pay at all.

Under this scenario, the family will have saved £67,418 (£98,000 - £30,582) in UK Capital Gains Tax.

Before we leave this subject, however, I have two very important words of warning.

Firstly, as explained in Section 1.3, a non-UK resident individual remains chargeable to UK Capital Gains Tax on assets which they employ in a UK business.

Secondly, as discussed in the 'Scope of this Guide', a non-UK resident may be subject to foreign tax on future capital gains.

See also Section 11.2 regarding the potential consequences arising when a UK resident transferee subsequently emigrates.

Chapter 8

Transfers into Trust

8.1 KEEPING CONTROL

As we have seen, direct transfers to other individuals have three major limitations: you cannot retain control of the asset yourself; you cannot create a gain by transferring it to your spouse; and you generally cannot transfer an asset directly to a minor child.

One of the best answers to these limitations is to use a trust; especially when considering non-business assets and property.

In effect, when using a trust, you are able to retain control over transferred assets by being a trustee of that trust.

A lifetime transfer of assets into trust will create a capital gain in much the same way as a transfer to another individual. Many of the issues discussed in Chapter 7 therefore continue to be relevant.

Furthermore, the transfer will still create a capital gain along the same lines even if you, your spouse, or one of your minor children, is a beneficiary of the trust. Such trusts are known as 'settlor-interested trusts'.

If you use a settlor-interested trust, you personally will be taxed on any future capital gains or income arising in the trust, but the objective of creating a capital gain to be taxed at the current low rate will have been achieved.

Furthermore, by being a beneficiary of your own trust, you can even retain the income from the transferred assets.

A trust is also often useful where you wish to pass assets to adult children but do not yet want them to have full control over those assets.

8.2 TRUSTS AND HOLDOVER RELIEF

It is not possible to claim holdover relief on a transfer of any asset into a settlor-interested trust, an offshore trust (i.e. a non-UK resident trust), or a dual resident trust.

Subject to this, however, when transferring assets to any other trust, such as a UK resident trust for the benefit of your adult children, for example, you can usually claim holdover relief on **any asset!**

Furthermore, generally speaking, a holdover relief claim can usually be made when transferring an asset out of a trust and passing it directly to the ultimate beneficiary.

In this way, almost any asset can eventually be passed to a trust beneficiary (other than you, your spouse, or your minor children) free from Capital Gains Tax. This is why trusts are often a useful way to transfer non-business assets, including investment property.

Whether you actually want to claim holdover relief on the transfer into the trust is another matter. As we know, a holdover relief claim results in a reduction in the transferee's base cost and means that the historic growth in an asset's value is exposed to future Capital Gains Tax increases.

This is fine if the beneficiary is likely to retain the asset for many years to come, but it defeats the object of the exercise if we are trying to shelter the asset's current value from future Capital Gains Tax increases. These issues were discussed in detail in Section 7.5 and are equally relevant to holdover relief claims on transfers of assets into trust.

There are, however, two very important benefits arising from this general ability to make holdover relief claims on any assets transferred into trust.

Firstly, it means that the option to make sales at below market value, and thus use a partial holdover relief claim, exists for any asset transferred to a trust (unless you are using a settlor-interested trust). For further details on the benefits of partial holdover relief claims see Sections 7.6, 7.7 and 10.2.

Secondly, the ability to hold over the gain arising when assets eventually leave the trust means that you will later be able to pass assets directly to the trust beneficiary free from any further Capital Gains Tax charge.

This includes assets leaving a settlor-interested trust, so you could eventually use this mechanism to pass assets back to yourself or to your spouse. In other words, you cannot generally transfer assets into a settlor-interested trust free from Capital Gains Tax but, under current law, you should be able to get them out again without incurring any further Capital Gains Tax charge.

One word of warning though: all this is based on current law and could potentially be changed under the new Capital Gains Tax regime.

Note also that, as with holdover relief on transfers of business assets, any holdover relief claim made on a transfer of assets into, or out of, a trust, is irrevocable.

8.3 TRUSTS AND INHERITANCE TAX

A lifetime transfer into trust will generally be a 'chargeable lifetime transfer' for Inheritance Tax purposes.

The amount of the chargeable lifetime transfer is the market value of the transferred asset less any amounts which the trust pays for the asset and less any available annual exemption.

The Inheritance Tax annual exemption is a different exemption to the Capital Gains Tax annual exemption and amounts to £3,000 per tax year. Any unused part of the previous year's Inheritance Tax annual exemption can also be used so that, if no previous chargeable lifetime transfers have been made since 5th April 2009, up to £6,000 of a transfer made during 2010/11 may be exempt.

Example

Sanjeev has made no previous chargeable lifetime transfers. During 2010/11, he transfers a property to a settlor-interested trust. The trust pays £100,000 for the property, but it is worth £300,000. The amount of Sanjeev's chargeable lifetime transfer is as follows:

	£
Value of property transferred	*300,000*
Less:	
Amount paid by trust	*100,000*
2010/11 annual exemption	*3,000*
2009/10 annual exemption	*3,000*
Chargeable lifetime transfer	*194,000*

As you can see from the example, transfers into a settlor-interested trust are treated as chargeable lifetime transfers in the same way as other lifetime transfers into trust. This even applies if the transferor themselves is the only trust beneficiary!

If any individual makes chargeable lifetime transfers totalling more than the Inheritance Tax nil rate band in any seven year period, then the excess is immediately chargeable to Inheritance Tax at the rate of 20%.

The amount of the nil rate band used for this purpose is the amount applying at the end of the relevant seven year period. The nil rate band currently stands at £325,000 and, under current proposals, is not due to be increased until at least 6th April 2015.

Chargeable lifetime transfers taking place within the seven years prior to the transferor's death may be subject to additional Inheritance Tax at the time of death and may also give rise to increased Inheritance Tax liabilities on other transfers taking place during the same period (including potentially exempt transfers – see Section 7.9) and on the deceased's estate.

Chargeable lifetime transfers taking place within the seven years before that (i.e. between seven and fourteen years prior to the transferor' death) can also result in an increase in the Inheritance Tax liabilities on other transfers, including potentially exempt transfers, taking place in the seven years prior to death.

Hence, in short, chargeable lifetime transfers in excess of £325,000 will give rise to immediate Inheritance Tax charges and any chargeable lifetime transfers made in the previous fourteen years may lead to additional Inheritance Tax charges on the transferor's death.

Anniversary and Exit Charges

Inheritance Tax charges may also apply to assets held within a trust on every tenth anniversary of the trust's creation and on the occasion that those assets are transferred out of the trust. The maximum potential charge in each case is 6% of the value of the trust assets.

These charges can generally be avoided by keeping the transferor's total chargeable lifetime transfers to less than the amount of the nil rate band and then ensuring that the assets are transferred out of the trust within less than ten years.

For further details on all of the issues covered in this section, see the Taxcafe.co.uk guide *'How to Avoid Inheritance Tax'*.

8.4 AVOIDING INHERITANCE TAX

Subject to the points set out in the previous section, it will generally be possible to avoid any Inheritance Tax problems on transfers into trust by keeping the total value of the assets transferred to no more than £331,000.

This figure is made up of the current nil rate band plus two Inheritance Tax annual exemptions and is based on the assumption that the transferor has not made any previous chargeable lifetime transfers within the previous seven years.

Under the same principles, a couple holding assets jointly should generally be able to transfer assets worth a total of £662,000 if they structure it correctly.

If you wish to transfer assets worth more than these figures then, to avoid any immediate Inheritance Tax charge, the trust will need to make a partial payment in order to reduce the chargeable lifetime transfer down to the appropriate figure. The example in Section 8.3 demonstrates this principle in action.

Remember, however, that such partial payments represent actual consideration and may therefore give rise to Stamp Duty Land Tax liabilities on property (see Section 12.1) and Stamp Duty at 0.5% on shares.

8.5 TRUSTS AND INCOME TAX

For Income Tax purposes, trusts can be divided into three basic types:

- Settlor-interested trusts
- Interest in possession trusts
- Discretionary trusts

As explained in Section 8.1, the transferor is subject to Income Tax on any income received by a settlor-interested trust.

An interest in possession trust exists when a beneficiary has an automatic right to the income received by the trust. In this case, the beneficiary is subject to Income Tax on the income received.

In both of these cases, the trust income is simply treated as part of the individual's own income and normal Income Tax rates apply.

Discretionary trusts pay Income Tax in their own right. Subject to a small basic rate band of £1,000, these trusts now pay Income Tax at the 'super tax' rate of 50%.

Although some of the Income Tax can generally be recovered later by any beneficiary in receipt of income from the discretionary trust, this does suggest that one should think twice before transferring high-income bearing assets into such a trust!

8.6 TRUSTS AND CAPITAL GAINS TAX

As explained in Section 8.1, transferors are personally subject to Capital Gains Tax on capital gains arising in a settlor-interested trust.

In other cases, the trust itself generally pays Capital Gains Tax on any sales or other disposals of assets. As we know from Section 8.2, however, Capital Gains Tax can usually be avoided on transfers out of a trust.

Trusts are currently subject to Capital Gains Tax at the same flat rate of 18% as individuals. They also have an annual exemption equal to half of the annual exemption for individuals (subject to further reductions if the same transferor has also made transfers into other trusts).

It is worth noting, however, that under the pre-2008 Capital Gains Tax regime, trusts were subject to Capital Gains Tax at 40% (subject to the same reliefs and exemptions as were available to individuals, including taper relief).

It is therefore quite possible that the same will apply under the new Capital Gains Tax regime.

8.7 TRUSTS AND PRINCIPAL PRIVATE RESIDENCE RELIEF

It is important to note that principal private residence relief (see Section 1.5) cannot be claimed on a property on which holdover relief has previously been claimed on a transfer into, or out of, a trust.

However, by transferring residential property into a trust without making any holdover relief claim, it may be possible to avoid Capital Gains Tax on any future capital gain on the property by allowing a beneficiary of the trust to use it as their principal private residence.

Chapter 9

Transfers to a Company

9.1 KEEPING IT ALL

Our final method for creating a capital gain is to transfer assets into a company. This is particularly useful as a means of creating a Capital Gains Tax 'disposal' of a business – often known as 'incorporation'.

Transfers of businesses and other qualifying assets into a company can often be carried out free from Capital Gains Tax.

However, as we shall see later in this chapter, it will not usually be beneficial to claim exemption on the transfer of assets into a company unless the assets are to be retained for the foreseeable future, or at least replaced by other assets within the company.

In other cases, there will be the usual Capital Gains Tax cost on the original transfer but, thereafter, the asset will be protected from any increase in Capital Gains Tax rates.

In the case of property, however, there is a major drawback in the shape of Stamp Duty Land Tax. We will look at this further in Section 9.4.

9.2 INCORPORATION

There are two ways to transfer a business into a company free from Capital Gains Tax.

Firstly, holdover relief is available for gifts or sales at below market value of qualifying business assets to a company. The qualifying conditions are much the same as in Section 7.5, except that holdover relief cannot be claimed on a transfer of shares to a company.

The consequences of a holdover relief claim for the transferor will be exactly the same as described in Sections 7.5 to 7.7, but the position for the transferee company will be totally different since it is subject to an entirely different tax regime, as we shall see in Section 9.3.

Secondly, a transfer of a business to a company in exchange for shares in that company is eligible for a different form of relief, known as 'incorporation relief' (see Sections 1.5 and 9.10). The whole business and all its assets must generally be transferred.

A form of partial incorporation relief can be achieved by transferring a business in exchange for a mixture of shares and cash consideration (which, as usual, can be left outstanding as a loan if required).

In theory, **any** type of business is eligible for incorporation relief. It is certainly available for trading businesses, professional activities and furnished holiday letting businesses (assuming that the furnished holiday letting regime is still in force – see Section 3.4).

It may also be available for other property businesses, although this is far from certain. For a detailed discussion of this point, see the Taxcafe.co.uk guide *'Using a Property Company to Save Tax'*.

Both holdover relief and incorporation relief are extremely useful when you wish to transfer a business into a company free from Capital Gains Tax with the expectation of running the business and retaining the relevant assets within the company for the foreseeable future.

However, as we shall see later in this chapter, the reliefs are less likely to provide any benefit when you anticipate selling the transferred assets within a few years.

Note that, where the relevant conditions are met, incorporation relief is automatic and does not need to be claimed. Hence, if you do not want the relief to apply, it must be disclaimed (see Section 10.2).

9.3 CAPITAL GAINS IN COMPANIES

Companies do not pay Capital Gains Tax. Instead, they pay Corporation Tax on their capital gains.

A company's capital gains are simply added to its income and the combined sum is then subjected to Corporation Tax at the usual rates applying.

Generally speaking, the effective rates of Corporation Tax paid by trading companies or property investment companies are currently as follows:

Income and Gains Rate

First £300,000	21%
£300,000 to £1,500,000	29.75%
Over £1,500,000	28%

These rates have to be adjusted if the company has any active associated companies or has an accounting period of any duration other than twelve months.

Other investment companies generally pay Corporation Tax at 28% on all income and capital gains.

Reliefs and Exemptions

Companies are still eligible for indexation relief which exempts the purely inflationary element of capital gains, based on movements in the Retail Prices Index.

Companies are also eligible to claim rollover relief, as described in Section 1.5, and may set capital losses off against capital gains arising in the same accounting period or a later one.

However, companies do not get an annual exemption and nor are they eligible for any of the other reliefs described in Section 1.5.

Future Capital Gains in Companies

The new coalition Government has promised a major reform of Corporation Tax and has stated that Corporation Tax rates will be 'reduced and simplified' over the next five years.

As yet, this is all we know, but it does suggest that the Corporation Tax rates applying to capital gains in companies in the future are likely to be considerably lower than the future Capital Gains Tax rates applying to higher rate taxpayers.

9.4 STAMP DUTY LAND TAX ON TRANSFERS TO COMPANIES

When any property is transferred to a 'connected company' (see Section 2.5), the company must pay Stamp Duty Land Tax based on the market value of the property, regardless of whether any actual consideration is paid.

The 'linked transactions' rules will also apply, meaning that Stamp Duty Land Tax rates of up to 4% will often apply. See Section 12.1 for further details.

9.5 POTENTIAL SAVINGS

As usual, I will demonstrate the potential savings which might be achieved by way of an example.

This example is based on the following assumptions:

- The Capital Gains Tax regime will remain unchanged for the remainder of the 2010/11 tax year.
- Thereafter, Capital Gains Tax will be charged at Income Tax rates, except that the 50% 'super tax' rate will not apply.
- The annual exemption will be reduced to just £5,000 from 2011/12 onwards.
- The 'small companies rate' of Corporation Tax applying to the first £300,000 of a company's income and gains will be reduced to 20%.

Example

David is a higher rate taxpayer. He has an investment property which is currently worth £250,000, but which he purchased for just £100,000 some years ago.

David transfers the property into Tannten Limited, his own property investment company.

David realises a capital gain of £150,000 on the transfer. After deducting his annual exemption of £10,100, the remaining £139,900 is subject to Capital Gains Tax at 18%, giving David a tax bill of £25,182 due in January 2012.

Tannten Limited pays Stamp Duty Land Tax at 1% (see Section 12.1) of £2,500, giving it a base cost of £252,500 for the property.

A few years later, the property is sold for £350,000. Inflation, according to the Retail Prices Index, has totalled 25% over the intervening period, so the company's capital gain is calculated as follows:

	£
Sale proceeds	350,000
Less:	
Base cost	252,500
Indexation relief	
£252,500 x 25%:	63,125
Capital gain	34,375

Assuming that the company's total income and gains for the relevant accounting period do not exceed £300,000, the Corporation Tax payable on this capital gain, at 20%, will be just £6,875.

If David had still held the property personally at this time, his capital gain would have been as follows:

	£
Sale proceeds	350,000
Less:	
Base cost	100,000
Annual exemption	5,000
Taxable gain	245,000

David's Capital Gains Tax bill, at 40%, would therefore have been £98,000.

At this stage, it looks like the transfer has saved David £63,443 (£98,000 less the £25,182 in Capital Gains Tax that he paid on the transfer, the £2,500 in Stamp Duty Land Tax paid by the company and the £6,875 in Corporation Tax paid on the ultimate sale).

If he now invests in another property, or other assets, held by Tannten Limited then this saving will effectively be retained: for the time being at least.

But, if he now wants to withdraw his sale proceeds from the company, he faces a few problems.

9.6 PROFIT EXTRACTION PROBLEMS

As we saw in the previous section, a transfer of assets into a company could save a considerable amount of tax when the assets are ultimately sold: even without any holdover relief on the initial transfer.

However, after paying the Corporation Tax bill, the net sales proceeds will still be sitting in the company. If the owner of the company now wants to get his or her hands on this money, they have to find a way of extracting it.

If the company is still needed for other investments, the usual choices for extracting the net sale proceeds are a dividend or a salary. A salary will seldom be appropriate in this situation, but a great deal more information on this issue can be found in the Taxcafe.co.uk guide *'Salary versus Dividends'*.

A higher rate taxpayer is subject to Income Tax at an effective rate of 25% on dividends; increasing to 36.1% where their total taxable income for the year exceeds £150,000 (and that 'total taxable income' has to include the one ninth tax credit attached to the dividends themselves).

Hence, in our example in the previous section, David could face an Income Tax bill of up to £123,906 if he extracted the net sale proceeds of £343,125 (£350,000 - £6,875) from Tannten Limited by way of dividend.

This would be disastrous, but the position would be drastically improved if David had transferred the property into the company in the right way in the first place.

9.7 DON'T GIVE, SELL!

For non-business assets, where it is not possible to claim any form of holdover relief, there is no point in giving the assets to the company. Instead, you should sell the assets to the company at their current market value.

This will make no difference to the amount of Capital Gains Tax arising on the transfer, nor to the amount of Stamp Duty Land Tax due, and you can leave the purchase consideration outstanding as a loan from you to the company.

For a transfer of shares, it will mean a small additional cost of 0.5% in Stamp Duty but this will generally be a price worth paying.

Repaying the Loan

The reason this is all so beneficial is that, when the underlying assets are eventually sold by the company, you can repay yourself the amount of the original loan and this sum does not need to be included as income for Income Tax purposes: it is simply a capital repayment.

There may still be an Income Tax cost if you wish to extract the profit element of the sale proceeds, but it will be drastically reduced.

Example Continued
(See Section 9.5 for background and assumptions)

Let us now assume that David originally sold his property to Tannten Limited for its full market value of £250,000 and the purchase consideration was left outstanding as a loan. David also loaned the company a further £2,500 to pay the Stamp Duty Land Tax bill, making a total loan balance of £252,500.

After selling the property, the company was left with net sale proceeds of £343,125 (£350,000 - £6,875). It uses this to repay David's loan, leaving a balance of £90,625.

David therefore only needs to extract £90,625 by way of dividend, giving him an Income Tax bill of somewhere between £22,656 (at 25%) and £32,726 (at 36.1%).

David's final overall net saving after extracting the net sale proceeds from the company will therefore be between £30,717 (£63,443 - £32,726) and £40,787 (£63,443 - £22,656).

9.8   OBSOLETE COMPANIES

If you no longer need your company for other investments after selling the transferred assets, then another alternative may be to wind the company up rather than pay yourself a dividend.

As in Section 9.7, the amount of any loan repayment can be excluded from the amount paid to you on the winding up, but the remainder would be treated as sale proceeds subject to Capital Gains Tax. From this, you would be able to deduct any amount that you paid for your company shares, i.e. your base cost.

At present, is not possible to say whether this would work out better than paying yourself a dividend. Under the current Capital Gains Tax regime, it is generally a considerably cheaper option than a dividend, but how these two methods will compare in the future is unknown.

9.9   POTENTIAL SAVINGS WITH HOLDOVER RELIEF

As we know, Capital Gains Tax can often be avoided on the original transfer of qualifying business assets into the company, but this may prove to be less beneficial in the long run.

Example Revisited
(See Section 9.5 for background and assumptions)

Let us now assume that David's property was a qualifying furnished holiday let and that the furnished holiday letting regime still applies at the time of his transfer (see Section 3.4).

David is therefore able to gift the property and to claim holdover relief, thus avoiding the initial Capital Gains Tax bill of £25,182.

The company will still pay Stamp Duty Land Tax of £2,500, however, giving it a base cost of £102,500 for the property (£100,000 + £2,500).

The company's capital gain on the ultimate sale of the property is now calculated as follows:

	£
Sale proceeds	350,000
Less:	
Base cost	102,500
Indexation relief	
£102,500 x 25%:	25,625
Capital gain	221,875

Assuming that the company's total income and gains for the relevant accounting period do not exceed £300,000, the Corporation Tax payable on this capital gain, at 20%, will be £44,375.

At this stage, David has made a net saving of £51,125 (the £98,000 in Capital Gains Tax which he has avoided less Corporation Tax of £44,375 and Stamp Duty Land Tax of £2,500).

However, this is not as good as the net saving of £63,443 which we saw in Section 9.5.

Furthermore, David still has the problem of how to extract the net sale proceeds from the company and he has no loan balance to deduct.

In summary, it may not make sense to hold over the original capital gain on a transfer of assets to the company if you anticipate selling the assets within the foreseeable future.

Furthermore, in this instance, David might have reduced his original Capital Gains Tax bill on the transfer to just £13,182 by claiming entrepreneurs' relief, thus eventually yielding an overall net saving of £75,443 by **not** claiming holdover relief.

Finally, as discussed in Section 7.5, it is also worth reflecting that any asset which is eligible for holdover relief may also be eligible for some form of exemption under the new Capital Gains Tax regime.

This casts some doubt over whether it is actually worth transferring such assets into a company at all.

9.10 POTENTIAL SAVINGS WITH INCORPORATION RELIEF

As explained in Section 9.2, for a transfer of a whole business into a company, there is an alternative form of holdover relief called 'incorporation relief'.

This relief may be claimed where qualifying business assets are transferred in exchange for shares in the recipient company. The effect is to exempt the transferor from Capital Gains Tax on the transfer and give them a base cost in their shares which is effectively equal to their base cost in the transferred assets.

The company's base cost in the transferred assets will be the market value of those assets at the date of transfer, thus achieving a tax-free uplift in base cost to current market value (and no-one had to die).

To demonstrate the potential savings available, we will return to our usual example.

Example Revisited (Again)
(See Sections 9.5 and 9.9 for background and assumptions)

Let us now assume that David transferred his qualifying furnished holiday letting property to his company in exchange for shares and claimed incorporation relief on the transfer in order to avoid Capital Gains Tax.

The company's base cost for the property will once more be £252,500, as in Section 9.5, i.e. its market value at the date of transfer plus the Stamp Duty Land Tax paid.

Hence, on the subsequent sale of the property, the company's Corporation Tax bill will again be £6,875 (see Section 9.5).

At this stage, subject to any exemptions which might have applied under the new Capital Gains Tax regime (see Section 3.6), David has saved £88,625 (the £98,000 of Capital Gains Tax he has avoided less £6,875 in Corporation Tax and £2,500 in Stamp Duty Land Tax).

This is the best saving that we have seen and is therefore the ideal result if David is content to reinvest the sale proceeds within the company for the foreseeable future.

He could extract the net profit of £90,625 (£350,000 - £252,500 - £6,875) by way of a dividend, giving rise to an Income Tax bill of between £22,656 and £32,726 (see Section 9.7). This would still leave him with a saving of between £55,989 (£88,625 - £32,726) and £65,969 (£88,625 - £22,656).

However, assuming that the company has no other way to generate distributable profits, in order to extract the rest of his sale proceeds David would have to either wind up the company or apply for a reduction in share capital: a complex business either way.

David would then end up subject to Capital Gains Tax under the new regime on the original held over capital gain of £150,000. This could possibly amount to up to £60,000 (at 40%), thus leaving David with a final overall net saving of just £5,969 at best, or an overall net additional tax cost of £4,011 at worst.

Once again, it is clear that claiming exemption from Capital Gains Tax on the initial transfer of assets into the company is unlikely to be very beneficial in the long run if you plan to sell those assets within the foreseeable future and are not content to reinvest the proceeds within the company.

If you are content to reinvest your sales proceeds within the company then claiming incorporation relief may prove advantageous.

However, the whole question of whether it is worth transferring assets eligible for incorporation relief into the company in the first place is again subject to the question of whether you might have been eligible for some form of exemption on those assets under the new Capital Gains Tax regime if you had simply retained them yourself (as discussed in Section 9.9).

Chapter 10

What If It Goes Wrong?

10.1 SAFETY NETS

In view of all the uncertainties which we discussed in Chapter 3, it would be nice to be able to create a capital gain now, on the basis that it may be beneficial to do so, but then undo our planning if it turns out to be unnecessary, or even disadvantageous.

Luckily, in a few situations, it is possible to do this and, in this chapter we will look at these 'safety nets': the instances where a gain created now can be wholly or partly 'undone' later.

There are two important provisos to all this, however.

Firstly, undoing the tax planning will not also undo all of the costs and other practical problems which we looked at in Chapter 4.

Secondly, the techniques described in this chapter are based on current legislation and could be blocked under the new Capital Gains Tax regime.

10.2 THE HOLDOVER OPTION

The time limit for claiming holdover relief on a gift or sale at below market value of qualifying business assets is three years after the 31st January following the end of the relevant tax year. In other words, for a qualifying transfer taking place during 2010/11, you have until 31st January 2015 to make a holdover relief claim.

The same time limit applies to holdover relief claims on a transfer of any assets into a trust.

Hence, where you have made a transfer of qualifying business assets to another individual or a company, or a transfer of any assets to a trust (except for a settlor-interested trust), you will have several years to decide whether you actually want to create the capital gain or not.

Note that where you make a sale at below market value, you will not be able to hold over the element of the gain based on the actual sale proceeds (see Section 7.6). This does enable you to design your own 'safety net', however. In other words, sell the asset for an amount which gives rise to a capital gain which you are sure that you want and leave yourself the option of holding over the remaining capital gain if this proves to be beneficial.

By way of illustration, take a look at the examples in Sections 7.6 and 7.7. Both Barbara in Section 7.6 and Leila in Section 7.7 are in the position of being effectively able (with Susan and Navin's agreement respectively) to choose between creating a smaller gain, using holdover relief, or a larger gain without it if this proves more beneficial.

This is particularly useful for Leila in Section 7.7. By claiming holdover relief, she can restrict her capital gain to the amount which qualifies for entrepreneurs' relief and is taxed at an effective rate of just 10%. However, if it later proves more beneficial to create the whole potential gain of £7m, including £5m taxed at 18%, she can simply choose not to make the holdover relief claim.

Note that, once made, a holdover relief claim is irrevocable so, if you're hoping to use this 'safety net', you need to wait until you know the position before you make your holdover relief claim.

The same principles apply to a holdover relief claim on a transfer to a company, which may be particularly useful given the issues which we discussed in Chapter 9.

The time limit for disclaiming incorporation relief (see Section 9.2) is generally two years after the 31st January following the end of the relevant tax year. Hence, for a transfer taking place, during 2010/11, you will generally have until 31st January 2014 to disclaim the relief.

However, this time limit is accelerated by a year if you dispose of all of your new shares before the end of the tax year after the transfer.

10.3 THE REINVESTMENT OPTION

As explained in Section 1.5, it is possible to defer the gain arising on the sale of certain business assets, including trading premises, goodwill and furnished holiday letting properties (provided that the furnished holiday letting regime still applies – see Section 3.4) by reinvesting the sale proceeds in new qualifying business assets.

The reinvestment needs to take place within three years after the original sale.

Hence, if you create a capital gain by selling a qualifying business asset, you could avoid Capital Gains Tax by reinvesting your sale proceeds in new qualifying assets at any time within the next three years.

This provides you with a suitable 'escape plan' if it turns out that creating the capital gain was not such a good idea after all!

10.4 RE-ACQUIRING SHARES

As explained in Section 6.2, a re-purchase of company shares within 30 days after a disposal of the same class of shares in the same company means that you are treated as if the new shares are the ones that you disposed of.

This applies equally to both quoted and unquoted shares and, in some cases, may provide the opportunity to 'undo' some tax planning which appears to have backfired.

Example

Matt owns 10,000 shares in RTD plc which he originally acquired for just £1 per share, but which are now worth £21 per share. Matt has already used his annual exemption for 2010/11.

Fearing an increase in Capital Gains Tax rates, Matt sells his shares on 15th June 2010, realising a capital gain of £200,000 and giving him a Capital Gains Tax liability, at 18%, of £36,000 under the current regime. Matt hopes that this will yield him a good long-term saving.

Unfortunately, on 22nd June 2010, it is announced that the increased Capital Gains Tax rates will apply from 6th April 2010 [just for the purposes of this example].

Matt's gain will now be taxed at 40%, giving him a liability of £80,000 and very little prospect of any long-term saving.

On 29th June 2010, Matt therefore repurchases 10,000 shares in RTD plc for £21 per share.

As this is within 30 days of his original sale, Matt is now treated as if the new shares are the ones that he sold on 15th June. He has therefore successfully eliminated his capital gain and has no Capital Gains Tax to pay.

Note that, in the example, Matt was able to repurchase his shares at the same price that he sold them for.

In reality, this will seldom be the actual position for quoted shares and hence either some gain will still be left, or a capital loss will arise. However, most of the Capital Gains Tax liability is still likely to be eliminated in the vast majority of cases.

10.5 CREATING CAPITAL LOSSES

If you have any assets standing at a loss, an open market sale of those assets within the same tax year can be used to reduce the Capital Gains Tax liability on your capital gains.

Hence, if you create a capital gain during 2010/11, you can reduce your Capital Gains Tax liability by making open market sales of loss-making assets at any time up until 5th April 2011. Generally speaking, however, you would only benefit by doing this if you do not have any other assets which are likely to be exposed to higher rates of Capital Gains Tax in the future.

If you do have any such assets then deferring a sale of your loss-making assets would generally make sense as the value of your loss relief will be greater in the future.

See also Section 12.4 regarding capital losses on transfers other than open market sales.

Chapter 11

Other Planning Issues

11.1 FURNISHED HOLIDAY LETTING

As explained in Section 3.4, furnished holiday letting currently enjoys a special tax status and this may possibly continue under the new Capital Gains Tax regime. The current qualifying conditions for a property to enjoy this status are set out below. It is important to bear in mind, however, that these may be 'tightened up' in the future.

Current Qualifying Conditions

The current qualification requirements for a property to be regarded as a furnished holiday letting are as follows:

i) The property must be situated in the European Economic Area (see Appendix B).
ii) The property must be furnished (to at least the minimum level which an occupier would usually expect).
iii) It must be let out on a commercial basis with a view to the realisation of profits.
iv) It must be available for commercial letting to the public generally for at least 140 days in a 12-month period.
v) It must be so let for at least 70 such days.
vi) The property must not normally be in the same occupation for more than 31 consecutive days at any time during a period of at least seven months out of the same 12-month period as that referred to in (iv) above. This seven month period need not be a single continuous period but must include the lettings under (v) above.

The 12-month period referred to in (iv) and (vi) above is normally the UK tax year but special rules apply in the years in which letting commences or ceases.

A taxpayer with more than one furnished holiday letting property may use a system of averaging to determine whether they meet test (v).

Whilst the property need not be in a recognised holiday area, the lettings should strictly be to holidaymakers and tourists in order to qualify.

Where a property qualifies, as set out above, then it generally qualifies for the whole of each qualifying tax year, subject to special rules for the years in which holiday letting commences or ceases.

For further information on all aspects of the current furnished holiday letting regime, see the Taxcafe.co.uk guide *'Furnished Holiday Lets: Your Emergency Tax Planning Guide'*.

11.2 EMIGRATION

Individuals facing substantial Capital Gains Tax liabilities sometimes avoid them by emigrating. As explained in Section 1.3, non-UK resident individuals are not generally subject to UK Capital Gains Tax.

If the Capital Gains Tax rate on many assets increases from 18% to 40% or more, there will be many more people for whom this course of action becomes worthwhile.

However, merely going on a world cruise for a year will not be sufficient, as it is necessary to become non-UK ordinarily resident, as well as non-UK resident.

This is a complex field of tax planning. However, the key points worth noting are:

- Emigration must generally be permanent, or at least long-term (usually at least five complete UK tax years).
- Disposals should be deferred until non-residence has been achieved.
- Limited return visits to the UK are permitted.
- Returning prematurely to the UK, to resume permanent residence here, may result in substantial Capital Gains Tax liabilities.
- It is essential to ensure that there is no risk of inadvertently becoming liable for some form of capital taxation elsewhere. (There is no point in 'jumping out of the frying pan and into the fire!')

Emigration to avoid UK tax is a strategy which is generally only worth contemplating when the stakes are high. Naturally, therefore, detailed professional advice is always essential.

The following example illustrates the broad outline of what is involved.

Example

Lea has been a highly successful UK property investor for many years. By early 2011, she has potential Capital Gains Tax liabilities on her UK investment property portfolio of over £2,000,000.

She therefore decides to emigrate and, on 3rd April 2011, she flies to New Zealand where she settles down to a new life.

During the 2011/12 UK tax year, Lea sells all her UK properties, but is exempt from Capital Gains Tax as a non-resident. Eventually, however, she decides that she wants to return home and, on 8th April 2016, she comes back to the UK to live.

As Lea was non-resident for over five complete UK tax years, she should be exempt from Capital Gains Tax on all her property sales.

Notes to the Example

i) I picked New Zealand because I happen to know that there is no Capital Gains Tax there. Nevertheless, it is always essential to take detailed local professional advice in the destination country.

ii) The sales giving rise to capital gains must be deferred until the next UK tax year after the tax year of departure.

iii) If Lea had returned to the UK to live before 6th April 2016, all of her property disposals in 2011/12 would have become liable to UK Capital Gains Tax. The gains would then be treated as if they had arisen in the tax year in which Lea returned to the UK. I guess you can put up with a lot of homesickness for £2,000,000.

Return Visits

Limited return visits to the UK are permitted. The general rules on return visits are:

- They must not exceed 182 days in any one UK tax year.
- They must average less than 91 days per year.

From 6th April 2008, any day on which you are present in the UK at midnight is counted for the purpose of the above tests (unless you are merely in transit from one foreign country to another).

However, this is only one aspect of the situation and must be regarded as the minimum criterion for maintaining non-resident status. In practice, HM Revenue and Customs will look at many other factors and the more links that the emigrant maintains with the UK the more likely they are to continue to be UK resident or ordinarily resident and hence still liable for Capital Gains Tax.

Holdover Relief and Emigration

If an individual becomes neither UK resident nor UK ordinarily resident then any held over capital gains on assets which they acquired within the previous six UK tax years become chargeable to Capital Gains Tax.

There are some exceptions if the individual's non-residence is only temporary and arises by reason of their employment or an office they hold.

Chapter 12

Problem Areas

12.1 STAMP DUTY LAND TAX

Stamp Duty Land Tax is currently payable on the total of the actual or deemed consideration paid for a property at the following rates:

Consideration	Rate Applying
Residential property up to £125,000	Nil
Commercial property up to £150,000	Nil
All property in excess of the above but not exceeding £250,000	1%
£250,001 to £500,000	3%
Over £500,000	4%

The previous Labour Government also proposed to introduce a new rate of 5% for residential property in excess of £1,000,000 with effect from 6th April 2011. It is currently unknown whether this proposal will go ahead.

Actual consideration includes any amount payable for the property, even amounts left outstanding as a loan. It also includes the outstanding balance on any mortgage or other loan over the property for which liability is assumed by the transferee.

There is no exemption for transfers between spouses.

Example

Ford sells a property to his wife Anna for £20,000 subject to her also assuming responsibility for the outstanding mortgage of £160,000.

The total consideration is therefore £180,000 and Anna must pay Stamp Duty Land Tax of £1,800 (at 1%).

Transfers to a Company

For transfers to a connected company, the actual consideration paid is disregarded and Stamp Duty Land Tax is payable on deemed consideration equal to the property's market value.

Linked Transactions

Where two or more properties are acquired from the same transferor at the same time, or as part of a single contract or other arrangement, the rate of Stamp Duty Land Tax will be based on the total consideration, or deemed consideration, for all of the properties.

This is a particular problem for landlords transferring property portfolios into a company.

12.2 THE PERILS OF PERSONAL USE

Any subsequent personal use of an asset by a transferor after a gift, sale at below market value, or transfer to a connected company, should generally be avoided. Such use may give rise to one or more of the following:

- Personal Capital Gains Tax liabilities on a subsequent sale of the asset
- Income Tax charges under the Pre-Owned Assets legislation
- Additional Inheritance Tax charges on a 'Gift with Reservation'
- Increased Corporation Tax charges
- Income Tax benefit in kind charges and Class 1A National Insurance costs
- Lost interest relief

Further information on these matters is provided in the Taxcafe.co.uk guides *'How to Avoid Inheritance Tax'* and *'Using a Property Company to Save Tax'*.

12.3 BUSINESS TRANSFERS

Any transfer of a sole trader business or the whole of your share in a trading partnership, whether to a company, another individual, or a trust, is treated as a cessation of business. This has numerous further tax consequences with many benefits, but also many pitfalls, to be aware of, so professional advice is essential.

12.4 TRANSFERS OF LOSS-MAKING ASSETS

As discussed in Section 10.5, an open market sale of a loss-making asset may be used as a means to reduce your Capital Gains Tax bill, although it may mean that you miss out on using the same loss to make greater savings in the future.

However, you should generally avoid making any other transfers of assets standing at a loss. Unless it's an arm's length sale to an unconnected person, the loss arising can only be set off against future gains on transfers to the same person, so it could be very difficult to get any relief for it.

12.5 REMITTANCE BASIS DRAWBACKS

As explained in Section 1.3, UK resident individuals who are either non-UK ordinarily resident or non-UK domiciled may claim the 'remittance basis' of taxation on both income and capital gains arising overseas.

This means that capital gains on disposals of foreign assets will only be subject to UK Capital Gains Tax if and when the proceeds are remitted to the UK.

However, from 2008/9 onwards, any individual with £2,000 or more of unremitted foreign income and capital gains who claims the remittance basis is subject to the following additional charges:

- Their Income Tax personal allowance is withdrawn
- Their Capital Gains Tax annual exemption is withdrawn
- Where they have been UK resident for seven or more of the previous nine UK tax years there is an additional fixed tax charge of £30,000

Appendix A

UK Tax Rates and Allowances: 2008/9 to 2010/11

	Rates	2008/9 £	2009/10 £	2010/11 £
Income Tax				
Personal allowance		6,035	6,475	6,475
Basic rate band	20%	34,800	37,400	37,400
Higher rate/Threshold	40%	40,835	43,875	43,875
Personal allowance withdrawal				
Effective rate/From	60%	n/a	n/a	100,000
To		n/a	n/a	112,950
Super tax rate/Threshold	50%	n/a	n/a	150,000
Starting rate band applying to interest and other savings income only				
	10%	2,320	2,440	2,440
National Insurance Contributions				
Class 1 – Primary	11%	) On earnings between earnings threshold and		
Class 4	8%	) upper earnings limit		
Earnings threshold		5,435	5,715	5,715
Upper earnings limit		40,040	43,875	43,875
Class 1 – Secondary	12.8%	- On earnings above earnings threshold		
Class 1 & Class 4	1%	- On earnings above upper earnings limit		
Class 2 – per week		2.30	2.40	2.40
Small earnings exception		4,825	5,075	5,075
Class 3 – per week		8.10	12.05	12.05
Pension Contributions				
Annual allowance		235,000	245,000	255,000
Lifetime allowance		1.65M	1.75M	1.8M
Capital Gains Tax				
Annual exemption:				
Individuals		9,600	10,100	10,100
Trusts		4,800	5,050	5,050
Inheritance Tax				
Nil Rate Band		312,000	325,000	325,000
Annual Exemption		3,000	3,000	3,000
Pensioners, etc.				
Age allowance: 65-74		9,030	9,490	9,490

Age allowance: 75 and over	9,180	9,640	9,640
MCA: born before 6/4/1935 (1)	6,625	6,965	6,965
MCA minimum	2,540	2,670	2,670
Income limit	21,800	22,900	22,900
Blind Person's Allowance	1,800	1,890	1,890

Notes
1. The Married Couples Allowance, 'MCA', is given at a rate of 10%. A lower allowance of £6,535 applied in 2008/9 where both of the couple were aged under 75 throughout the year.
2. The rates given for 2010/11 were correct at the time of publication but could be subject to subsequent changes.

Appendix B

The European Union & The European Economic Area

The European Union

The 27 member states of the European Union are:

Austria	admitted 1st January 1995
Belgium	founding member
Bulgaria	admitted 1st January 2007
Cyprus	admitted 1st May 2004
Czech Republic	admitted 1st May 2004
Denmark	admitted 1st January 1973
Estonia	admitted 1st May 2004
Finland	admitted 1st January 1995
France	founding member
Germany	founding member
Greece	admitted 1st January 1981
Hungary	admitted 1st May 2004
Irish Republic	admitted 1st January 1973
Italy	founding member
Latvia	admitted 1st May 2004
Lithuania	admitted 1st May 2004
Luxembourg	founding member
Malta	admitted 1st May 2004
Netherlands	founding member
Poland	admitted 1st May 2004
Portugal	admitted 1st January 1986
Romania	admitted 1st January 2007
Slovakia	admitted 1st May 2004
Slovenia	admitted 1st May 2004
Spain	admitted 1st January 1986
Sweden	admitted 1st January 1995
United Kingdom	admitted 1st January 1973

Any rights which citizens of countries admitted on 1st May 2004 or 1st January 2007 have under UK tax law commence on the date that their country was admitted to membership.

The European Economic Area comprises the 27 member states of the European Union plus Iceland, Liechtenstein and Norway.

Appendix C

Connected Persons

The definition of 'connected persons' differs slightly from one area of UK tax law to another. Generally, however, an individual's connected persons include the following:

i) Their husband, wife or civil partner
ii) The following relatives:
- Mother, father or remoter ancestor
- Son, daughter or remoter descendant
- Brother or sister

iii) Relatives under (ii) above of the individual's spouse or civil partner
iv) Spouses or civil partners of the individual's relatives under (ii) above
v) The individual's business partners
vi) Companies under the control of the individual or of any of their relatives under (i) to (iv) above
vii) Trusts where the individual, or any of their relatives under (i) to (iv) above, is a beneficiary

Appendix D

Indexation Relief Rates
(See Section 2.7 for details of the continuing application of this relief in certain circumstances)

Percentages applying to disposals made by individuals between 1 April 1998 and 5 April 2008 of assets acquired (or enhancement expenditure incurred) during:

Month	Rate	Month	Rate	Month	Rate
Mar-82	104.7%	Mar-85	75.2%	Mar-88	56.2%
Apr-82	100.6%	Apr-85	71.6%	Apr-88	54.5%
May-82	99.2%	May-85	70.8%	May-88	53.1%
Jun-82	98.7%	Jun-85	70.4%	Jun-88	52.5%
Jul-82	98.6%	Jul-85	70.7%	Jul-88	52.4%
Aug-82	98.5%	Aug-85	70.3%	Aug-88	50.7%
Sep-82	98.7%	Sep-85	70.4%	Sep-88	50.0%
Oct-82	97.7%	Oct-85	70.1%	Oct-88	48.5%
Nov-82	96.7%	Nov-85	69.5%	Nov-88	47.8%
Dec-82	97.1%	Dec-85	69.3%	Dec-88	47.4%
Jan-83	96.8%	Jan-86	68.9%	Jan-89	46.5%
Feb-83	96.0%	Feb-86	68.3%	Feb-89	45.4%
Mar-83	95.6%	Mar-86	68.1%	Mar-89	44.8%
Apr-83	92.9%	Apr-86	66.5%	Apr-89	42.3%
May-83	92.1%	May-86	66.2%	May-89	41.4%
Jun-83	91.7%	Jun-86	66.3%	Jun-89	40.9%
Jul-83	90.6%	Jul-86	66.7%	Jul-89	40.8%
Aug-83	89.8%	Aug-86	67.1%	Aug-89	40.4%
Sep-83	88.9%	Sep-86	65.4%	Sep-89	39.5%
Oct-83	88.3%	Oct-86	65.2%	Oct-89	38.4%
Nov-83	87.6%	Nov-86	63.8%	Nov-89	37.2%
Dec-83	87.1%	Dec-86	63.2%	Dec-89	36.9%
Jan-84	87.2%	Jan-87	62.6%	Jan-90	36.1%
Feb-84	86.5%	Feb-87	62.0%	Feb-90	35.3%
Mar-84	85.9%	Mar-87	61.6%	Mar-90	33.9%
Apr-84	83.4%	Apr-87	59.7%	Apr-90	30.0%
May-84	82.8%	May-87	59.6%	May-90	28.8%
Jun-84	82.3%	Jun-87	59.6%	Jun-90	28.3%
Jul-84	82.5%	Jul-87	59.7%	Jul-90	28.2%
Aug-84	80.8%	Aug-87	59.3%	Aug-90	26.9%
Sep-84	80.4%	Sep-87	58.8%	Sep-90	25.8%
Oct-84	79.3%	Oct-87	58.0%	Oct-90	24.8%
Nov-84	78.8%	Nov-87	57.3%	Nov-90	25.1%
Dec-84	78.9%	Dec-87	57.4%	Dec-90	25.2%
Jan-85	78.3%	Jan-88	57.4%	Jan-91	24.9%
Feb-85	76.9%	Feb-88	56.8%	Feb-91	24.2%

Appendix D (cont'd)

Month	Rate	Month	Rate	Month	Rate
Mar-91	23.7%	Aug-93	15.1%	Jan-96	8.3%
Apr-91	22.2%	Sep-93	14.6%	Feb-96	7.8%
May-91	21.8%	Oct-93	14.7%	Mar-96	7.3%
Jun-91	21.3%	Nov-93	14.8%	Apr-96	6.6%
Jul-91	21.5%	Dec-93	14.6%	May-96	6.3%
Aug-91	21.3%	Jan-94	15.1%	Jun-96	6.3%
Sep-91	20.8%	Feb-94	14.4%	Jul-96	6.7%
Oct-91	20.4%	Mar-94	14.1%	Aug-96	6.2%
Nov-91	19.9%	Apr-94	12.8%	Sep-96	5.7%
Dec-91	19.8%	May-94	12.4%	Oct-96	5.7%
Jan-92	19.9%	Jun-94	12.4%	Nov-96	5.7%
Feb-92	19.3%	Jul-94	12.9%	Dec-96	5.3%
Mar-92	18.9%	Aug-94	12.4%	Jan-97	5.3%
Apr-92	17.1%	Sep-94	12.1%	Feb-97	4.9%
May-92	16.7%	Oct-94	12.0%	Mar-97	4.6%
Jun-92	16.7%	Nov-94	11.9%	Apr-97	4.0%
Jul-92	17.1%	Dec-94	11.4%	May-97	3.6%
Aug-92	17.1%	Jan-95	11.4%	Jun-97	3.2%
Sep-92	16.6%	Feb-95	10.7%	Jul-97	3.2%
Oct-92	16.2%	Mar-95	10.2%	Aug-97	2.6%
Nov-92	16.4%	Apr-95	9.1%	Sep-97	2.1%
Dec-92	16.8%	May-95	8.7%	Oct-97	1.9%
Jan-93	17.9%	Jun-95	8.5%	Nov-97	1.9%
Feb-93	17.1%	Jul-95	9.1%	Dec-97	1.6%
Mar-93	16.7%	Aug-95	8.5%	Jan-98	1.9%
Apr-93	15.6%	Sep-95	8.0%	Feb-98	1.4%
May-93	15.2%	Oct-95	8.5%	Mar-98	1.1%
Jun-93	15.3%	Nov-95	8.5%	Apr-98	
Jul-93	15.6%	Dec-95	7.9%	or later	0.0%

Appendix E

Short Leases
(See Section 2.8)

Proportion of the original cost of a lease of 50 or more years' duration allowed as a deduction for Capital Gains Tax purposes on a disposal of that lease.

Years Remaining	%	Years Remaining	%
50	100	25	81.100
49	99.657	24	79.622
48	99.289	23	78.055
47	98.902	22	76.399
46	98.490	21	74.635
45	98.059	20	72.770
44	97.595	19	70.791
43	97.107	18	68.697
42	96.593	17	66.470
41	96.041	16	64.116
40	95.457	15	61.617
39	94.842	14	58.971
38	94.189	13	56.167
37	93.497	12	53.191
36	92.761	11	50.038
35	91.981	10	46.695
34	91.156	9	43.154
33	90.280	8	39.399
32	89.354	7	35.414
31	88.371	6	31.195
30	87.330	5	26.722
29	86.226	4	21.983
28	85.053	3	16.959
27	83.816	2	11.629
26	82.496	1	5.983

TAX Cafe®

Pay Less Tax!

...with help from Taxcafe's unique tax guides and software

All products available online at www.taxcafe.co.uk/books

Other popular Taxcafe titles include:

- *How to Avoid Property Tax*
- *Using a Property Company to Save Tax*
- *How to Avoid Tax on Foreign Property*
- *Furnished Holiday Lets: Your Emergency Tax Planning Guide*
- *How to Avoid Inheritance Tax*
- *How Couples Save Tax*
- *Master Property Capital Gains Tax in 2 Hours*
- *Property Capital Gains Tax Calculator (Software)*
- *Tax-Free Property Investments*
- *Salary versus Dividends*
- *Using a Company to Save Tax*
- *Selling Your Business*
- *Small Business Bookkeeping, Tax & VAT*
- *How to Beat the Recession*
- *The Investor's Tax Bible*
- *Non-Resident and Offshore Tax Planning*
- *The World's Best Tax Havens*
- *Tax Saving Tactics for Non-Doms*
- *How to Build a £4 Million Property Portfolio*

All products available online at www.taxcafe.co.uk/books

Disclaimer

1. Please note that this Tax Guide is intended as general guidance only for individual readers and does NOT constitute accountancy, tax, investment or other professional advice. Neither Taxcafe UK Limited nor the author can accept any responsibility or liability for loss which may arise from reliance on information contained in this Tax Guide.

2. Please note that tax legislation, the law and practices by government and regulatory authorities (e.g. HM Revenue and Customs) are constantly changing. We therefore recommend that for accountancy, tax, investment or other professional advice, you consult a suitably qualified accountant, tax specialist, independent financial adviser, or other professional adviser. Please also note that your personal circumstances may vary from the general examples given in this Tax Guide and your professional adviser will be able to give specific advice based on your personal circumstances.

3. This Tax Guide covers UK taxation only and any references to 'tax' or 'taxation' in this Tax Guide, unless the contrary is expressly stated, refer to UK taxation only. Please note that references to the 'UK' do not include the Channel Islands or the Isle of Man. Foreign tax implications are beyond the scope of this Tax Guide.

4. Whilst in an effort to be helpful, this Tax Guide may refer to general guidance on matters other than UK taxation, Taxcafe UK Limited and the author are not expert in these matters and do not accept any responsibility or liability for loss which may arise from reliance on such information contained in this Tax Guide.

5. Please note that Taxcafe UK Limited has relied wholly on the expertise of the author in the preparation of the content of this Tax Guide. The author is not an employee of Taxcafe UK Limited but has been selected by Taxcafe UK Limited using reasonable care and skill to write the content of this Tax Guide.